Joomla! 1.5 JavaScript jQuery

Enhance your Joomla! sites with the power of jQuery extensions, plugins, and more

Jose Argudo Blanco

BIRMINGHAM - MUMBAI

Joomla! 1.5 JavaScript jQuery

First published: July 2010

Production Reference: 1190710

Published by Packt Publishing Ltd.
32 Lincoln Road
Olton
Birmingham, B27 6PA, UK.

ISBN 978-1-849512-04-6

www.packtpub.com

Cover Image by Asher Wishkerman (a.wishkerman@mpic.de)

Credits

Author
Jose Argudo Blanco

Reviewers
Eric Brown

Tahsin Hasan

Acquisition Editor
Darshana Shinde

Development Editor
Rakesh Shejwal

Technical Editor
Hithesh Uchil

Copy Editors
Janki Mathuria

Lakshmi Menon

Indexer
Hemangini Bari

Editorial Team Leader
Akshara Aware

Project Team Leader
Lata Basantani

Project Coordinator
Srimoyee Ghoshal

Proofreader
Aaron Nash

Graphics
Geetanjali Sawant

Production Coordinator
Aparna Bhagat

Cover Work
Aparna Bhagat

About the Author

Jose Argudo Blanco is a web developer from Valencia, Spain. After completing his studies, he started working for a web design company. Then, six years later, he decided to freelance.

Now that some years have passed as a freelancer, he thinks it's the best decision he has ever taken because it let him work with the tools that he likes, such as Joomla!, CodeIgniter, CakePHP, jQuery, and other well-known open source technologies.

His desire to learn and share his knowledge has led to him being a regular reviewer of books from Packt Publishing, including *Magento 1.3 Sales Tactics*, *Openx Ad Server*, *Drupal E-commerce*, *Joomla! With Flash*, *Joomla! 1.5 SEO,* and *Magento Theme Design*.

Recently, he published his own book, *CodeIgniter 1.7*, which you can also find on Packt's site. And since then he has been working on this Joomla! book, putting all his effort into it.

> To Silvia, my brother, my family, Packt's team, and, of course, to you, the reader. I hope this book is useful to you.

About the Reviewers

Eric Brown, born and raised in California, joined the US Navy at 17 and became a Preventive Medicine Technician. Upon exiting military service, he left the medical field behind and moved to Nebraska and entered college to study art and design, which resulted in a Bachelor's of Science in Graphic Design from Wayne State College in Nebraska. Eric has since branched out by teaching himself (or learning from others) various aspects of HTML, CSS, and PHP as well as a variety of other code languages and web marketing strategies and tools. He currently owns his own design and development business located in Curtis, Nebraska, where he lives with his wife and pets.

Over the years Eric has worked for a local design and development firm in Nebraska on such projects as the Golden Spike Tower website, aimed at tourist traffic centered on the Union Pacific's Bailey Yard, and with a premier pet industry design and development firm as a project manager. He has also written for such prestigious publications as Trafficology (a purchased print publication on web marketing read by over 80,000 worldwide), CMSWire.com (a leader in content management news), Revenews (a highly rated site on various aspects of marketing), and Gadgetell (a well-known gadget news site).

Eric has been involved in other books as well, providing editing, image touch-up, and custom hand-drawn maps for Tagging Along (a Neville Family retrospective) as well as editing, layout, cover art, and image touch-up for My Life and Community (autobiography of Ken Huebner).

I would like to thank any and all who have helped to bring my career to this point, but most of all I would like to thank my wife Jaime and two children Ariel and Autumn for all their patience and understanding as my career and business underwent their developmental stages.

Tahsin Hasan is the 16th Zend PHP 5 certified programmer from Bangladesh. He is a tech enthusiast and has more than five years of web development experience. He has proficiency in LAMP environment. Tahsin Hasan is deft in both client-side and server-side programming techniques. He has worked with several PHP frameworks, such as CodeIgniter, Symphony, and CakePHP. He has contributed several libraries to the CodeIgniter community. He has also worked on several jQuery plugins. He has professional experience on software development lifecycle.

Tahsin Hasan always contributes to technical discussions on cutting edge technologies on his blog (`http://newdailyblog.blogspot.com`). You can reach him at `tahsin352@yahoo.com`.

I would like to thank my parents and my siblings for their encouragement while reviewing this book. And I would like to give special thanks to Srimoyee Ghoshal, Project Coordinator at Packt Publishing.

Table of Contents

Preface

To date, Joomla! has been well known as a great content management system (CMS). There are many sites using it throughout the world, some of them having great features that impress their visitors. Most of the time, these appealing and powerful features work thanks to JavaScript. In this book, we are going to see how to enhance our site with these features, using another powerful open source tool—the jQuery JavaScript library.

Do you want to have a full-featured site? And more importantly, do you want to know how to develop jQuery-powered extensions? Just keep reading!

What this book covers

Chapter 1, Let's Start Making a Better Site – Images, shows how Joomla! works with images by default. It then moves on to explain some image slideshows, pop ups, and image galleries—all using some interesting Joomla! extensions, which are jQuery-powered.

Chapter 2, Site Content – Our Next Step, as its name suggests, is all about the content of our site and the different ways in which we can organize it. Not only does it show the basic ways, but also the use of tabs and article slideshows. It also includes a bit of site search, even AJAX site search.

Chapter 3, Embedding Rich Media Features with Joomla! Plugins, shows some interesting plugins, such as the code highlighter and Flickr plugins. We will also see the SC jQuery plugin—a plugin that will be of help in the future chapters of the book.

Chapter 4, One Last Look at Joomla! jQuery Modules, is where we will stop and see some interesting modules before proceeding to more complex chapters. For example, we will build drop-down menus, first with CSS and then with a Joomla! module. We will also see how to interestingly place the login module.

Chapter 5, Refactoring Our Site, is the last chapter before we start coding ourselves. Here we will stop and see how to make fewer jQuery library loads, and also some tips and warnings—it may not be the easiest chapter, but is an important one.

Chapter 6, Getting Our Hands on Coding JavaScript, shows us how to, instead of using Joomla! extensions, make use of some jQuery plugins to add some interesting effects to our template. This will involve some coding, but the results will be quite nice, including a Parallax effect, tooltips, and the always useful jScrollPane plugin.

Chapter 7, Creating Our Own Modules, shows us that it's much better to create our own modules so that our hard work of development can be easily used in any Joomla! site. In this chapter, we will see how to create our own modules with a small example: a quick, AJAX-powered contact form.

Chapter 8, Building Complete Solutions, Modules, and Components, will help us dive further and start working on a component. By the end of the chapter, we will not only have a working component backend, but also a module on the frontend to show our data—of course, with some interesting jQuery effects.

Chapter 9, Going Further with Our Component Development, continues work on our previous component to give it a frontend. However, we will also add some interesting features to the backend, such as textarea autogrow, equal size columns, pagination with JavaScript, and many more.

Chapter 10, Problems and Usability, is a chapter centered on solving some problems, and gives some interesting tips that we can apply to all the work we have seen throughout the book. It will cover topics such as JavaScript being unavailable and a failed AJAX request.

What you need for this book

Basic knowledge on Joomla! will help you follow the book. We try to make all explanations as easy to follow as possible. Basic HTML, PHP, and JavaScript knowledge is a prerequisite for the book. But don't worry, you will be provided with step-by-step explanations throughout the book. You will find this book very easy to follow. Also, in order to make the book even more easier to follow, you can download the code bundle from Packt's site. In the code bundle given on the site, you will find all the code that are given as examples in the book.

Who this book is for

This book is mostly for PHP developers who work with Joomla! and web designers
who want to add JavaScript and jQuery elements to their Joomla! themes and
modules. However, it will also be useful to those who are interested in building
their own jQuery-powered Joomla! extensions.

Conventions

In this book, you will find a number of styles of text that distinguish between
different kinds of information. Here are some examples of these styles, and an
explanation of their meaning.

Code words in text are shown as follows: "After we create an instance of the
controller class, we call the `execute` method."

A block of code is set as follows:

```php
<?php
defined( '_JEXEC' ) or die( 'Restricted access' );

jimport('joomla.application.component.controller');

class TinynewsController extends JController{

    function display(){
        parent::display();
    }

}
```

When we wish to draw your attention to a particular part of a code block, the
relevant lines or items are set in bold:

```php
class TinynewsController extends JController{

    var $_name='viewtoload';

    function display(){
        parent::display();
    }
```

New terms and important words are shown in bold. Words that you see on the screen, in menus or dialog boxes for example, appear in the text like this: "Then go to **Extensions | Install/Uninstall**. Here, after selecting the file, click on the **Upload file & install** button".

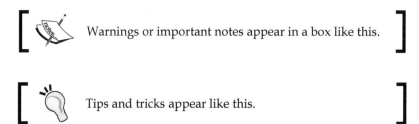

Warnings or important notes appear in a box like this.

Tips and tricks appear like this.

Reader feedback

Feedback from our readers is always welcome. Let us know what you think about this book—what you liked or may have disliked. Reader feedback is important for us to develop titles that you really get the most out of.

To send us general feedback, simply send an e-mail to feedback@packtpub.com, and mention the book title via the subject of your message.

If there is a book that you need and would like to see us publish, please send us a note in the **SUGGEST A TITLE** form on www.packtpub.com or e-mail suggest@packtpub.com.

If there is a topic that you have expertise in and you are interested in either writing or contributing to a book on, see our author guide on www.packtpub.com/authors.

Customer support

Now that you are the proud owner of a Packt book, we have a number of things to help you to get the most from your purchase.

Downloading the example code for the book

You can download the example code files for all Packt books you have purchased from your account at http://www.packtpub.com. If you purchased this book elsewhere, you can visit http://www.packtpub.com/support and register to have the files e-mailed directly to you.

Errata

Although we have taken every care to ensure the accuracy of our content, mistakes do happen. If you find a mistake in one of our books—maybe a mistake in the text or the code—we would be grateful if you would report this to us. By doing so, you can save other readers from frustration and help us improve subsequent versions of this book. If you find any errata, please report them by visiting `http://www.packtpub.com/support`, selecting your book, clicking on the **let us know** link, and entering the details of your errata. Once your errata are verified, your submission will be accepted and the errata will be uploaded on our website, or added to any list of existing errata, under the Errata section of that title. Any existing errata can be viewed by selecting your title from `http://www.packtpub.com/support`.

Piracy

Piracy of copyright material on the Internet is an ongoing problem across all media. At Packt, we take the protection of our copyright and licenses very seriously. If you come across any illegal copies of our works, in any form, on the Internet, please provide us with the location address or website name immediately so that we can pursue a remedy.

Please contact us at `copyright@packtpub.com` with a link to the suspected pirated material.

We appreciate your help in protecting our authors and our ability to bring you valuable content.

Questions

You can contact us at `questions@packtpub.com` if you are having a problem with any aspect of the book, and we will do our best to address it.

1
Let's Start Making a Better Site—Images

"Pictures are worth a thousand words; images are one of the best ways to make our site interesting and grab our visitors' attention."

Although some people will agree with this statement more than others, the truth is that images have been one of the most important aspects of websites to date. From images incorporated into the layout to images used in content, they all help to make our site look interesting and appealing. And that's very, very important. We can have the best content, products, and articles; however, if our site is not appealing enough, our visitors will leave before we can even show them all of our site's great features.

If you stop to think about it, this makes a lot of sense. A good looking site denotes a good quantity of effort being put into it, and in the end it gives a sense of seriousness to our site or business, which makes our visitors more confident.

In this chapter we are going to work with images, and will make use of some Joomla! modules to give our site the extra appeal that it needs.

These are some very nice additions for any site. If you don't have a live site, you can try them with the sample template that is provided with the book code. For now, our site looks similar to the following screenshot:

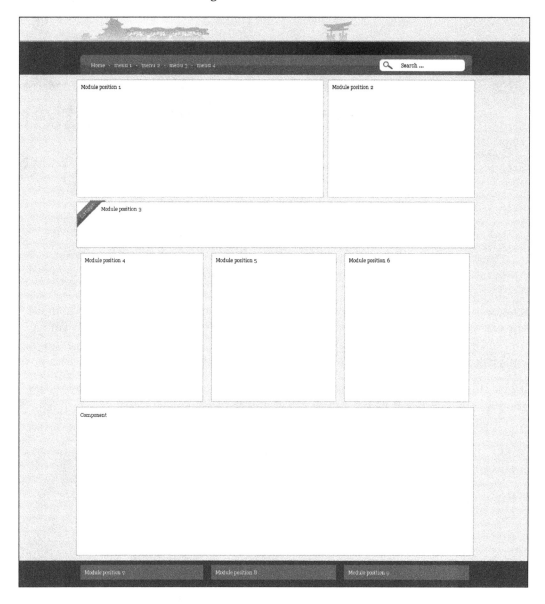

As you can see, there is a lot of work to be done on the layout mock-up. Let's see an overview of what we are going to cover in this chapter.

First, we will see how Joomla! handles images by default, without the help of any module or extension, using just Joomla! and images. Then, we will see some modules and extensions that will help us to:

- Add an image slideshow to our site
- Incorporate image pop ups—a great way of making our images stand out from our contents
- Create galleries

Through all of the examples in this book, we will look at jQuery-powered extensions to help us in our work. For now, let's stop talking and start working on our site.

How Joomla! handles images by default

Even though these basic ways of putting images onto our site won't make our site stand out from the competition, we are going to take a look at them. This will also show us the improvement achieved once we have used some of the modules previously commented on.

Inserting images into articles

Let's add an image to one of our content articles. Log in to your Joomla! Administration zone. Go to the **Media Manager**, and then to **stories**. Once you are there, upload an image.

For this example, we will be using the following image:

This image is named `image_1.png`. You can find it in the code for Chapter 1 in the code bundle of the book. Then go to **Content | Article Manager**; here we will create a sample article. Don't worry about the structure; it's not important for now. Create the article in the **Uncategorised** section and category:

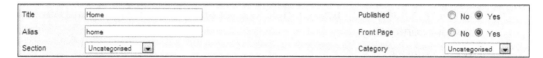

To insert the image into the article, click on the **Image** control button at the bottom of the editor (action **1**). Then, select the image (action **2**) and click on the **Insert** button (action **3**). The image is now inserted into the editor at the location where the cursor was placed. The actions involved are displayed in the following screenshot:

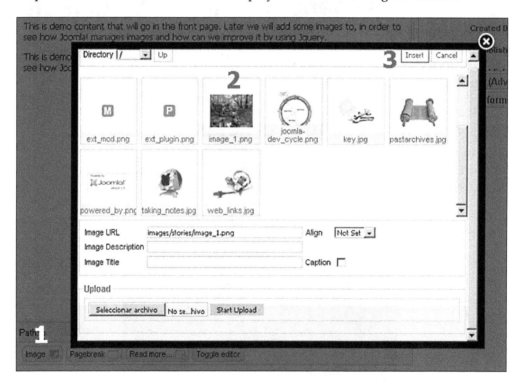

If all has gone OK, the result will be an image inserted into our article—nothing more, and nothing less. Do you want to see it? The result is as follows:

An image, like the one we have used, can make the article more interesting and is easy to incorporate.

Placing images in modules

Placing images in modules works in the same way as placing them in articles. However, images end up in module positions, and therefore you can use them as banners, ads, or something equally useful. For this example, we are going to use image_2.png (the following image), which is included in the code bundle. Don't forget to upload it to our Joomla! installation before continuing:

To create a module, go to **Extensions | Module Manager | New | Custom HTML**, and give the module a name you want. In this example, we will be placing the module in the **module_1** position.

As we have selected the **Custom HTML** module type, we will be presented with a WYSIWYG editor, similar to the one we had when creating the previous article. Insert the image as we have done before, and then save the module. When this is done, and if the module is published, the result will be similar to the following screenshot:

For now, this will be enough. Later, we will continue working with this module position. However, before that let's take a look at the process of placing images.

Placing images in the template

Most templates use images in the layout in order to make them more interesting; and, of course, our example template is no exception! To see how this is done, open your Joomla! installation folder. Go to the `templates` folder, and then to our `jj15` template folder.

Note that we are opening the `jj15` folder as it's the name of our template. Now open the `index.php` file and search for the following piece of code:

```
<div id="header">
    <img src="<?php echo $this->baseurl ?>/templates/jj15/
        images/header_image.gif" />
</div><!-- End of header -->
```

This will result in our header image being shown, as follows:

To get this to work, we have used the typical HTML `<img>` tag and a bit of PHP scripting, such as `<?php echo $this->baseurl ?>`, to generate the base URL of our site. This will, therefore, produce the following code:

```
<img src="/jj15/templates/jj15/images/header_image.gif" />
```

That's it! Enough of the basics. We want to make our site very interesting, so let's use jQuery for further improvement of our site along with the use of third-party extensions.

One of the most interesting features of working with Joomla! is that there are lots of extensions already built. These extensions will surely help us in the development of our site, saving time and effort, and will give great results in no time. In this chapter, we are going to take a look at some interesting Joomla! extensions.

 To take a look at all of the extensions available, you can go to:
`http://extensions.joomla.org/`

Don't worry, later in the book we will also see how to create our own extension. But don't go so fast my friend, stay with me and we will go step by step and create a very interesting site.

Adding a jQuery-powered image slideshow module

Slideshow is one of my favorite effects, and there are many Joomla! modules available to achieve this effect. For example, take a look at **AJAX Header Rotator**, which is available at `http://extensions.joomla.org/extensions/photos-a-images/images-rotators/10036`.

Or, you can simply perform a search in the **Joomla! Extension Directory (JED)** for "AJAX header rotator" and download the module—do so now, so that you can follow the example. After downloading the ZIP file, go to **Extensions | Install/Uninstall**, select the file, and click on **Upload File and Install**. After installing the file, on navigating to **Extensions | Module Manager** you will see that the **AJAX Header Rotator** module is still not enabled, so we will enable it.

Next, we are going to upload some images. You can upload any image whose dimensions are 587 x 257 px. However, if you wish, you can use image_3.png and image_4.png provided in the code bundle.

Navigate to the **Media Manager**, then to the stories folder, create a folder called module_1, and upload the images to this folder. After uploading the images, we can return to **Extensions | Module Manager** and open our **AJAX Header Rotator** module. Here you will see the module parameters, as shown in the following screenshot:

Let's go through these parameters:

- **Unique ID for this AJAX Header Rotator** — is important if we need more than one instance of this module.

- **Image Folder path** — is a very important parameter as it indicates the location of the folder where the images are placed. The images that we place in this folder will be the ones used by the module. In our example, we are going to use `images/stories/module_1` as the path.

- **Rotation speed** and **Rotation timeout** — will control the speed between image fades and the time for which each image is being shown. It's stated in milliseconds.

- **Image width** and **Image height** — well, these are very self explanatory; we will go for **587** x **257**px as the size of the images in our example. That is also the size of our module in the template. However, we could state any dimensions that we need in these parameters.

For now, we are not going to use links in the images, so leave the other parameters at their default values. Before saving these changes, remember to select the module position value to **module_1**, as we will use this in our example.

On refreshing our site, you will see something similar to the following screenshot:

I've tried to capture the very moment of the transition between two images. However, you will surely see it better on your own Joomla! installation, so why don't you try it?

Some other modules to try

Let me suggest some slideshow modules in case you would like to try them out. You can find all of them by searching the JED:

- **RokSlideshow** — is one of my favorite modules. Although it uses MooTools instead of jQuery, it has more effects and transitions. You should really try this module.
- **ImageSlideShow** — works in the same way as the module that we have seen in our example.
- **JT SlideShow** — is also jQuery-based, but also offers some nice features, such as pause-on-hover, auto-stop, auto-fit, before/after callbacks, and also some transitions to choose from.

Image pop ups

Using image pop ups is another way of making our site interesting, and is very common these days. You can see this effect in almost every site. So our site is not going to be lighter on effects than others; we are going to incorporate image pop ups, and in an easy way as you will see.

First we are going to download the module from `http://extensions.joomla.org/ extensions/multimedia/multimedia-display/4577`.

You can also search the JED for "Ninja ShadowBox". Once we have downloaded the file, we can install it, as always, by navigating to **Extensions | Install/Uninstall**. In the field where it says **Package File** you will click on **Select file**. In my installation, the file is called `mod_ninja_shadowbox-2.0.9.zip`. Select the file and click on **Upload File and Install**. Although the version number can change, the installation process will remain the same.

When the installation process finishes, we can find this extension under **Extensions | Module Manager**. At first, we may assume that this extension, as it behaves more like a plugin, would be found in the **Plugin Manager**, but no, this extension can be found in the modules section.

In this section, we will find a module called **Ninja ShadowBox**. Click on it to open its admin section (shown in the following screenshot):

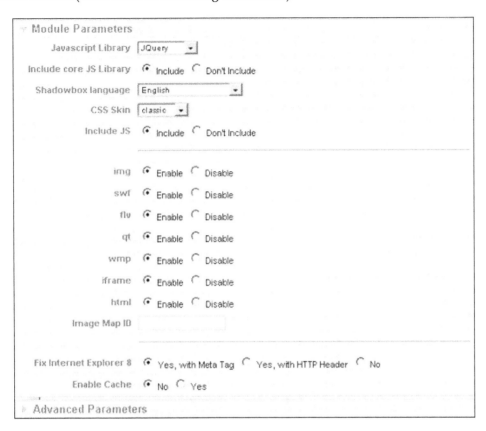

We could leave these parameters at their default values, and the module would work correctly. However, let's take a look at them:

- **Javascript Library** — lets us select which JavaScript library we are going to use. As the book is about Joomla! and jQuery, I think we will be leaving the default option, jQuery.

- **Include core JS Library** — can be set to **Don't include** if you are loading your own library in the template. Your library would be used instead of the ones provided by the module. Otherwise, this parameter could be left at its default value.

- **Shadowbox language** — provides lots of languages from which we can select our favorite. For the purposes of the example, I will be using the default selection of **English** as the language. However, please select your favorite language here.

- **CSS Skin** — is an important parameter, as it affects how the images are shown. For now, we are going to leave it as it is, but later you can come back here and change it.

- **Include JS** — relates to the shadowbox library. However, if you are going to use your own library (if there is a newer version or for some other reason) you can disable this parameter. For now, we'll be leaving this parameter as it is.

- **Media formats** — shows all of the media formats available. If you don't want to use some of them, you can disable them here. However, there's no need to do that for now.

- **Image Map ID** — is used to link image maps to images by placing the ID in this field. It is a parameter that we are not going to use.

- **Fix Internet Explorer 8** — lets us emulate the IE 7 behavior. Sometimes, code that worked well in IE 7 and other browsers may not work in IE 8. For me, the first option is working well, but you can change it if it's not working for you. This option generates the following line in the template:

```
<meta http-equiv="x-ua-compatible" content="IE=EmulateIE7" />
```

So our browser will try to emulate IE 7's way of rendering pages.

- **Enable Cache** — is a very useful parameter to use cache on a working site. However, as we are still in a development environment, we will leave this option at **No** — its default value.

Let's continue and see what we need to do in our articles to get this module to work. You may be thinking "But Jose, there's an Advanced Parameters tab!" — I know my friends, it's just that I want to show you many other things and don't have the space for all of it!

Anyway, the advance options are to be left at the default values. You need to enable them by selecting **True** in **Use Advanced Mode**. Later, when we finish this topic, I recommend you come back here and try all of these options. We don't need them now, but they can be interesting if you wish to give them a try.

Now save the module and go to **Content | Article Manager**.

Remember that in order for the module to work, we have to enable it. The position doesn't really matter as the module is not going to show anything in the module position.

Any article would be good for us. However, I'm going to use the one we created previously—you can use any other one though. After opening the article, add the following text to the end of it:

```
Click to open the image
```

Then click on the **Insert/edit link** button. A form similar to the following screenshot will open:

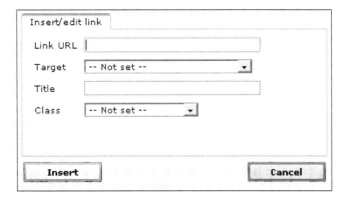

In the **Link URL** field we will enter the following path:

```
images/stories/image_1.png
```

This will create the link to the image, as we can see in the following screenshot.

However, when we click on this link we will be directed to another page, where we will be able to see the image. This is not the expected result, and that's because we still need to perform some tasks.

Well, in fact, we only need to modify the link code generated by the editor. So go back to the article editor, and click on the **HTML** button, as shown in the following screenshot:

This will open the source code editor, but don't worry, the changes needed are very easy to achieve. First, we need to find the link code. As of now, it will look more or less similar to the following:

```
<p><a href="images/stories/image_1.png">Click to open the image</a>
</p>
```

The tiny change required in this code is as follows:

```
<p><a href="images/stories/image_1.png" rel="shadowbox">Click to open
the image</a></p>
```

That's it, we have only added `rel="shadowbox"`.

Now apply the changes or save the article, go to the frontend, refresh the page, and click on the link again. If all has gone OK – and it should have – the image will pop up over the article. It should look similar to the following screenshot:

Remember that we can change the CSS skin and thus change the way the pop up will look. In order to do so, we only need to go back to the module admin skin, and select a different one.

Looks nice doesn't it? But we are not limiting the possibilities to only pop-up images. For example, take a look at the following code:

```
<p><a href="images/stories/image_1.png" rel="shadowbox[gallery]">Click
to open the image</a></p>
```

Using this code, in more than one image, we can create an image gallery with arrows to browse the images both forwards and backwards. However, try writing the following code:

```
<p><a href="http://www.google.com" rel="shadowbox">Click to open
google</a></p>
```

A pop up with the Google website inside will appear. As you can see, the possibilities are almost endless.

Some other modules to try

Of course, Ninja Shadowbox is not the only module that can help us with image pop ups. If we search the JED, we will find many other modules that can suit our needs. Take a look at the following modules:

- **BK-Thumb** — is a good module, and has lots of features, such as watermarking images, resize images, and many others — it seems only to work with images though.
- **YOOeffects** — is for the MooTools library, and works mostly in the same way. However, it can also add some other effects, such as reflection, to our pages.

Putting images together—image galleries

In this last part of the chapter, we are going to take a look at image galleries. Image pop ups are a very good option, but when we need to show a number of images, galleries are a better option. This time, we are going to use a very new plugin available at `http://extensions.joomla.org/extensions/photos-a-images/photo-gallery/10809`, which will help us in building the gallery.

As always, we can also perform a search for "pPGallery" in the JED. After we download it, we need to go to **Extensions | Install/Uninstall**, select the file, and upload it.

Once we have it installed, we need to go to **Extensions | Plugin Manager** and enable the plugin. Now navigate to the **Plugin Manager** and look for **Content – pPGallery**. Click on it to open its administrative panel.

First, we will enable the plugin—before we forget. And next, let's take a look at the parameters that the plugin provides, as shown in the following screenshot:

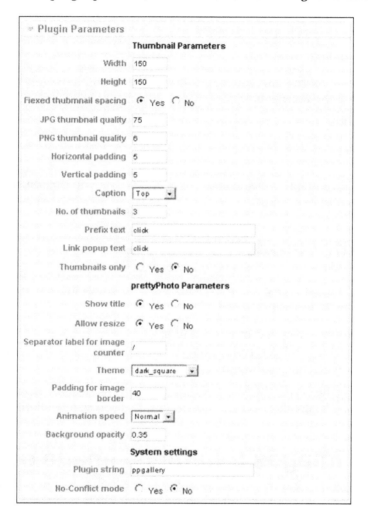

The parameters are listed as follows:

- **Width** and **Height**—will define the height and width of the thumbnails that will be shown on the front page.
- **Fixed thumbnail spacing**—will define the same amount of space between portrait images and landscape images.

- **Quality** — sums up the next two parameters for JPG and PNG thumbnail quality. These are for defining the quality of the thumbnails. We can leave these parameters at their default values.

- **Horizontal padding** and **Vertical padding** — are parameters that could also be defined in our CSS files. Defining these parameters here is also convenient.

- **Caption** — is used if images have `alt` tags in them to show captions. Here we can define the position of those captions. We can leave this parameter at its default value as we are not going to use captions for now.

- **No. of thumbnails** — is used if we don't want to show all of the images until the gallery pop up is opened. We can enter the number of thumbnails that we need to show in this field. In this example we have entered **3**.

- **Prefix text** — is the text that will appear before the descriptions of the images.

- **Link popup text** — is the text that will appear as links text in the images.

- **Thumbnails only** — is used if we don't want to use the pop-up gallery, and if we only want to have the thumbnail images, we can select **Yes** in this parameter. For our example, leave this at its default value.

Next, you will find the parameters for the pop-up image gallery. You can try them out later and modify them as you wish. However, for now, leave them at the default values. I've separated the next two parameters because one of them will help us with the appearance, and the other with possible problems:

- **Theme** — is used to change the style of the gallery.

- **No-Conflict mode** — can be set to **Yes** if you are having problems with other libraries. For now, we can leave it at its default value.

In order to save the changes, click on the **Save** icon. Now, let's move on to the interesting part, that is, to try the gallery! Open any article in the **Article Manager.** For this example, we are going to use the one we created earlier in this chapter.

And here comes the magic; where we want the gallery to be created, place the following code:

```
{ppgallery}/stories/ppgallery{/ppgallery}
```

Here you can see that the {ppgallery} tag needs to be used. Between the opening and closing tags, we will place the folder where our images are placed. You can use any folder, but of course, you will need it to have images. In the code bundle of the book, in the Chapter 1 subfolder, you can find another subfolder named ppgallery. I have placed some images in there for you to try. I hope you like them!

By default this plugin searches inside the `images` folder, and so we need to place `/stories/ppgallery` (where `ppgallery` is the sample folder where I have placed the images). You will need to change these values in your own installation.

After saving these changes, and refreshing the frontend, you will see something similar to the following screenshot:

As you can see, three images are shown, and this can be changed by modifying the **No. of thumbnails** parameter in the plugin administration skin. Now, if we click on an image, a pop up will open, with the full-size version of that image, as shown in the following screenshot:

At the bottom of the image we can see some arrows. If we take a look at it, we can now see that there are six images in total, though in the gallery we could see only three of them. This is because the folder /stories/ppgallery has six images, but we have selected only three in the parameters of the module to be shown. In our article, only three images are shown (as indicated by the parameter). However, in the gallery pop up all of the images can be viewed.

If you encounter any problem while using this plugin, it may be due to one or more extensions using the jQuery library simultaneously, or if the jQuery library is loaded after our plugin is loaded. For example, consider the following sequence of events:

1. Load of the jQuery library.

2. Load of the pPgallery script.

3. Load of another instance of the jQuery library, used by another extension.

In this case, the gallery will not work. The gallery script needs to be loaded after the jQuery library is loaded because the gallery script extends the jQuery library. If another Joomla! extension then loads another jQuery instance, without the addition of the gallery script, it will end up with the removal of the gallery script that was previously added.

In order to solve this, try to find out which extension is interfering. For example, in our case, the module "Ninja Shadowbox" may be causing the problem. To solve it, we only need to change the parameter **Include core JS Library** to **Don't include**. It should now work perfectly.

As we have seen, this is a very easy-to-use plugin, and a very helpful one too. It will help us show a group of images or form a gallery in just a few clicks.

Some other extensions to try

Again, I would like to show you some extensions that you can find in the JED:

- **Simple Image Gallery** — is a very interesting option. Though it uses MooTools, I recommend you to check it out, as it offers some interesting options.

- **Art Pretty Photo** — can show images from flicker, and also lets us create our own image thumbnails. We can even play videos with this plugin, which would be a very nice option too.

Tips and tricks

Now we are going to see some interesting tips and tricks. Don't miss them, because they can be very useful:

- Did you know that the Ninja Shadowbox module will resize the images according to browser size? We can therefore upload good quality images, with a good size, as visitors with smaller screen resolutions will also view the entire image without needing to use the scrollbars.

- To use a plugin, for example, the gallery plugin we have just seen, within a module, we need to use an extension such as the **Plugin In Module**. Check it out, it can come in handy at any time.

- While developing, take frequent backups so that you always have some working copies of the site. An extension that I like is Akeeba backup.

Summary

I hope this has been an interesting chapter for you. At first we had a look at how Joomla! works with images by default. Later, we worked with images in other interesting ways, such as image slideshows, pop ups, and galleries.

Go ahead and try them out now! I will be waiting for you in Chapter 2, in which we will work with site content such as:

- Article slideshows
- Putting content into tabs
- AJAX search

These are just a summary of what we are about to see, interesting isn't it? See you there soon!

2
Site Content—Our Next Step

"Site content is usually our main concern when developing a site, and can directly affect our success."

As we saw in the previous chapter, images can attract visitors and in the first instance itself make them stay on our site. We saw how to make these images more interesting and also how to take full advantage of them. But in the long run, content is what makes our visitors stay or return to our site.

Although we are not going to see how to prepare good content for our site, we will see how to organize them in some interesting ways. We are going to focus on topics, such as:

- Tabs—organizing our contents into tabs
- Article slideshows
- Site search—introducing AJAX searches

Quite interesting, isn't it? Keep reading!

Organizing our content into tabs can be very useful. It provides the ability to have more information placed in minimum amount of space, and is great for news and article introductions. We can also organize the content into slideshows; these work very much like image slideshows, but we will use them to show articles. Site search is as important as having good site content so that our visitors are able to find them. Although Joomla! has a great search feature, we will try to make it a bit more appealing.

Now let's get started!

Basic concepts on Joomla! content

First, let us start by taking a quick look at how Joomla! organizes and works with content. By default, in version 1.5, Joomla! organizes content into sections, categories, and articles. Sections and categories are used to organize our site content, which is represented by our articles.

Of course, we can have articles placed in uncategorized sections and categories. However, personally, I prefer to create a structure that maintains all of the site's content in an organized manner.

We will now create a section called "News". Navigate to your Joomla! Administrator screen, and then to **Content | Section Manager**. On this screen, we need to click on the **New** button, which will open the **Section** creation screen. On this screen, we can introduce the **Section** name and save it:

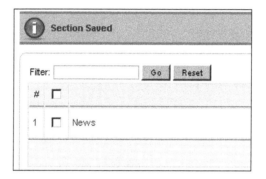

Now, inside this section, we will create two categories. Navigate to **Content | Category Manager** and click on the **New** button. Create the following two categories and remember to select **News** as the section that they belong to:

- Site News
- F.A.Q.

Once created, these categories will be listed as shown in the following screenshot, and as you can see they belong to the **News** section:

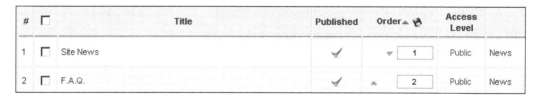

#		Title	Published	Order▲ ⚙		Access Level	
1	☐	Site News	✔	▼	1	Public	News
2	☐	F.A.Q.	✔	▲	2	Public	News

Well, we are now going to create some articles in these categories, just to have some articles to play with. We don't need to create very elaborate articles, just some Lorem Ipsum ones. Create them as you wish and then proceed to the next topic.

How Joomla! shows our articles to site visitors

The blog style is one of the basic ways in which we can display our articles. This style will show our articles in a structured fashion—it is very organized and quite interesting. I've created a blog menu with the articles inside our **Site News** category.

 Remember, in order to create this you need to navigate to **Menus | Main Menu | New | Articles | Category Blog Layout** and then configure the parameters as per your requirements.

Our site, more or less, will look similar to the following screenshot:

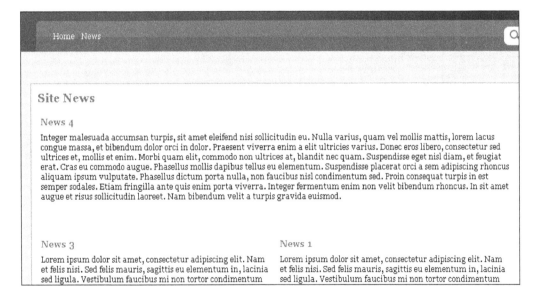

As you can see, most of the modules have disappeared, and our visitors can fully concentrate on the content that they are searching for. We can achieve this from each module's admin screen in **Extensions | Module Manager**.

Every module has a **Menu Assignment** zone to select where the module will appear. The options provided are:

- **All** — for the module to appear on every page of our site
- **None** — for the module not to appear
- **Select Menu Item(s) from the List** — for selecting where our module will appear

I've selected most of the modules to be displayed only on the **Home** menu, but feel free to select the option that suits your needs.

What can we do now with our articles? We can place them in some module positions in order to have them highlighted. Navigate to **Extensions | Module Manager | New** and from the menu select **Newsflash**. Though there are some other options, such as **Latest News**, we will use **Newsflash**. In the following screenshot, you can see the options that we will select:

First, we will give the module a **Title** and call it **Latest News**. Next, for this module, we will select **module_2** of our sample template as the module **Position**. Then, for the **Category**, select **News/Site News**, and also set the **Layout** as **Vertical**.

We could have chosen the **Horizontal** layout. In this case, our news would have appeared in columns instead of being placed one on top of the other.

For now, we are not going to show images and will only display the text of our articles. The last important parameter to change is **# of Articles**. In our example, we have set it to **4**. That's all we need; the other parameters can be configured any way we want. As a result, we will see something similar to the following screenshot on the front page:

To the right-hand side we can see our **Newsflash** module with four articles taken from the **Site News** category. Though this is an easy way of showing our articles in a module position, we can make it better. And this is what we are going to do in the next section.

Enhance your site content using JavaScript

We are going to use some Joomla! extensions to help us add some spice to our site. In keeping with the last example, we are first going to try to show our latest news in an article position.

Organizing our content into tabs

For this example, I would like to show you a simple, but very interesting extension. It is called **jTabs**, and although it works in a different way, it will help us show news in tabs. First, search for it in the JED; searching for the name should work, and if not, here's the link:

```
http://extensions.joomla.org/extensions/style-a-design/tabs-a-
slides/8265
```

Once the extension has been downloaded, navigate to **Extensions | Install/ Uninstall**. Then select the file and click on the **Upload File and Install** button. Once installed, you can navigate to **Extensions | Module Manager** and find our newly installed module listed as **jQuery tabs module**. Let's open it to see the parameters provided (as shown in the following screenshot):

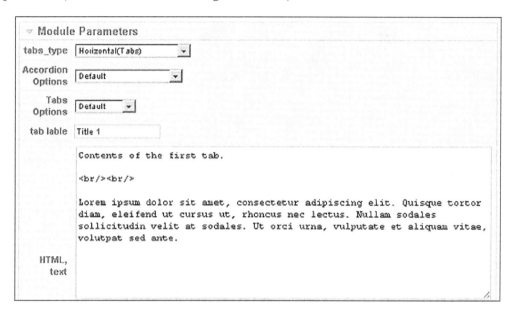

 Before publishing this module, don't forget to unpublish the other modules that occupy the **module_2** module position. Then publish this module in position **module_2**. This will ensure that only our new module occupies this position.

Let's check those parameters:

- **tabs_type** — is used to select **Horizontal(Tabs)** or **Vertical(Tabs).** For the first demo we are going to use the **Horizontal(Tabs)** option.

- **Accordion Options** — is used when we select **Vertical(Tabs)** in the previous parameter. Here you can select whether you want the tabs to be triggered when you click on them, or mouse over them.

- **Tabs Options** — works in the same way as the previous option, but for **Horizontal(Tabs)**. Therefore, we will be using this option in our example. Leaving the default option will work OK; so let's leave it as it is and continue to the next parameter.

- **tab lable** — is an option that lets us place the label or title that will appear on the tab.
- **HTML, text** — is used to place the text or HTML code that will go on the tab. We can place almost anything here, such as HTML code, JavaScript, and a lot more.

These last two parameters are repeated a number of times, letting us have nine tabs to use and giving us a lot of freedom of usage. Are you wondering how the module will look on our site? Check the following screenshot:

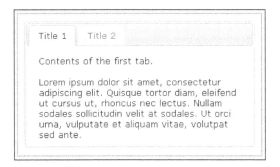

Looks interesting, but we can work on it a bit more with just two basic modifications to make it look better with the aesthetics of our site. First, we are going to remove the white box surrounding our module. This is very easy to achieve, just open the `templates/jj15/css/styles.css` file of our template. Look for the `#module_2` style and change the following code:

```
#module_2{
    background-image: url('../images/back_module_2.gif');
    background-repeat: no-repeat;
    float: right;
    width: 360px;
    height: 280px;
    overflow: hidden;
}
```

The modified code should look as follows:

```
#module_2{
    /*
    background-image: url('../images/back_module_2.gif');
    background-repeat: no-repeat;
    */
    float: right;
    width: 360px;
```

```
    height: 280px;
    overflow: hidden;
    margin-top: -22px;
}
```

Just one more step. Now, open the index.php file of the template and search for "<div id="module_2">". The code should be as follows:

```
<div id="module_2">
    <div class="pad">
      <jdoc:include type="modules" name="module_2" />
    </div>
</div><!-- End module 2 -->
```

Modify the code as follows:

```
<div id="module_2">
        <jdoc:include type="modules" name="module_2" />
</div><!-- End module 2 -->
```

In this way we are removing the padding that we were using before. Now our tabs module will use the entire space and will look a bit better. Imagine that we want to change the colors of the tabs, for example we want to make them white over a red background. Well, this can be very easy to achieve.

Just go to our site's modules folder, and there you will see the mod_jtabs folder and inside that a jquery folder. Here there are two important things to change:

- jquery-ui.css – is the CSS file where we can change the styles for the tabs
- images – is a folder that keeps the images used for this module

> We can take a shortcut by downloading a theme from the http://jqueryui.com/ site. Check it under the themes page, and select one of your liking – there are lots of them. Just for this example I'm going to use the one called "Blitzer". After downloading the theme, uncompress the ZIP file. Inside the css folder you will see a folder called Blitzer with a CSS file and another folder called images. This CSS file needs to be renamed to jquery-ui.css. Then, replace the CSS file and the images folder of our module with these new ones and there it is! Our changes are finished.

Now our tabs module will look more like the following screenshot:

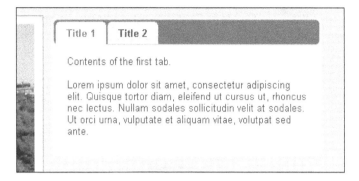

I think it's better now, hope you like it too! But anyway, why don't you try to change it to your liking? It's easy.

Some other modules to try

While working with this module I found some other interesting ones as well. Take a look at the following modules. As always you can search for them on the JED:

- **Simple jQuery Tabs**—may look similar, but this one will let us place modules in the tabs, instead of text or HTML code—it is very useful, don't miss it.

- **SlipTabs**—works with neither contents, nor modules, nor text. As you may be thinking, this module can be very interesting. It doesn't seem to be using jQuery, but anyway it's a very good choice.

- **RokTabs**—is a module that you shouldn't miss. It has some nice JavaScript effects and also uses MooTools. Therefore, it can work OK with any Joomla! installation.

Article slideshows

The article slideshow is one of my favorites. Like the tabs in the previous section, the article slideshow will help us in trying to show a large quantity of articles using minimum space possible. In the next example, we will see an interesting module that will show articles in a graceful slideshow and in an infinite loop.

First, as always, we need to download the extension we are going to use. This time we are going to work with the **Content Slider Module**. We can find it on the JED, or at the following link:

```
http://extensions.joomla.org/extensions/news-display/articles-
showcase/10444
```

After downloading the module, install it through the **Extensions | Install/Uninstall** screen. When the module is installed we can navigate to **Extensions | Module Manager**, and find it listed as **Content Slider Module**. We will now open the module (as shown in the following screenshot) and see the options provided:

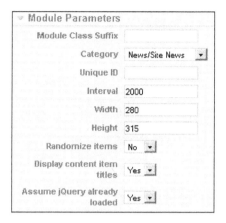

There are not many options this time, but enough for what we need. Let's take a look at them:

- **Module Class Suffix** – will let us write a suffix for the module, in case we need more power when styling our site. Adding a suffix will help us target this module better with our CSS classes.

- **Category** – is used to select the category from which the module will take the articles that will be shown on the front page.

- **Unique ID** – is required if we are going to use more than one instance of this module. We will need to assign a unique ID for each one.

- **Interval** – will establish the time interval between slides. The greater the number, the more time each slide will stay until the next one is loaded. If we don't want our visitors to hurry while trying to read the content inside each slide, we will need to place an appropriate number here.

- **Width** and **Height** – not much to say about these two. Here we can define the width and height of our module. For now, we can start with **280** px as the width and **315** px as the height.

- **Randomize items** – is an interesting option, but for now I will select **No**. However, you can modify it to see if it suits your needs.

- **Display content item titles** – is self-explanatory. For now, we will leave it as **Yes**.

- **Assume jQuery already loaded** – is a very useful option, and we will select **Yes** as we know that we already have another instance of jQuery loaded.

And that's all, but don't forget to enable the module before trying to see it on the frontend.

For this example I'm using the **module_4** module position, but you can use any other. Also, this is the only module that I've enabled in that position.

News 2

tur   Lorem ipsum dolor sit amet, consecte
elis   adipiscing elit. Nam et felis nisi. Sed f
inia sed   mauris, sagittis eu elementum in, lac
ortor   ligula. Vestibulum faucibus mi non t
ibulum.   condimentum vitae tristique leo vest

The previous image shows us how the module looks on the frontend. I've tried to capture the moment of change between slides. However, I encourage you to try it on your own to make it a bit more interesting. I have some images mixed along with some icons that my friends at Fairhead Creative prepared for me. You can find those images inside the folder for Chapter 2 in the code download. Do you want to see a preview? See the following screenshot:

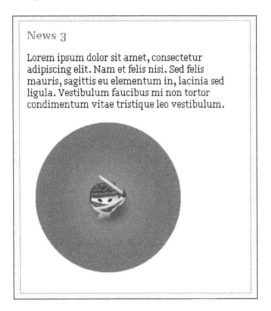

When we have all of the images placed we will have made a very neat effect. We may think that it is very similar to the image slideshow that we created in Chapter 1. However, this module has a very strong point; while keeping the interesting dynamic look and movement, we can have text in it. So our module will help us with SEO, as text is always better than images – for SEO I mean.

Some other extensions worth checking

Although the Content Slider Module extension suits our needs perfectly, there are other extensions that can help us in other occasions. Take a look at the following examples in the JED:

- **SlideShow** – has some nice features, like arrows that will let our visitors to move between slides.

- **YOOcarousel** – is a must, though it works with the MooTools JavaScript library. MooTools is the library that comes with Joomla! by default. You can check it out at `http://mootools.net/`; I really advise you to check it.

- **ChiBinhCMS - News Module** – is the perfect mix of images and text, though I think it requires a bit more space, it can be useful in certain templates.

Site search

It won't make much sense to have the best content in the world if our visitors couldn't search them. For small sites, a good menu structure could be OK. However, for medium or large sites, offering our visitors a search feature is a must, as many visitors will directly search for what they are looking for.

By default, Joomla! has a very powerful search feature that will search through all our site articles. We are going to take a look at this first. In the administrator screen go to **Extensions | Module Manager** and click on the **New** button. In the screen that will appear, click on **Search** (as we are creating a search module). We are going to name it **Basic Search** and we are going to place it in the **search** position of our template. After enabling it we can check how it looks on our frontend:

Though it doesn't look bad we can make some tweaks to make it look better.

Let's return to the module admin screen. We are going to add **_basicsearch** as the **Module Class Suffix**; this will help us with the styling of the module.

Once we have created the suffix we need to use it. For this we are going to open a CSS file in our editor. The file is located inside our template's `css` folder, and it's called (in a very original fashion) `styles.css`. Just add the following code to the end of the file:

```
/**
 * Basic search styles
 */

.inputbox_basicsearch{
  border: 0;
  margin-top: 5px;
}
```

And then, if we reload the frontend, we will see something similar to the following screenshot:

Better now, isn't it? Now when our visitors perform a search (for example, let's imagine that some of them are looking for an interesting topic on our site, like lorem ipsum — that's just a hot topic) they will be redirected to a screen that is similar to the following screenshot:

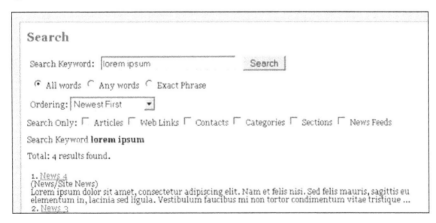

It will show our visitors all articles on our site that match this criteria. As you can see, it has only taken us a few minutes to prepare a fully working site search. However, there are ways in which we can make it better; just keep reading.

Introducing AJAX search

Imagine that our previous sample search gave no results. Our visitors will have to wait for the page to load, just to see that there are no results. Wouldn't it be better if we can show the results without redirecting? Much better I think, and that's exactly what we are going to do with AJAX search.

This time we are going to use the ajaxSearch module. Just search for it in the JED, or download it from the following link:

```
http://extensions.joomla.org/extensions/search-a-indexing/site-
search/8607
```

After the typical installation process, we will find the module in the **Extensions | Module Manager** screen. It will be called ajaxSearch. Open its admin screen, and we will take a look at its parameters.

 It appears that, by default, the module has the **Menu Assignment** set to **None**. We should change this to **All**, or a selection of menu options according to our needs.

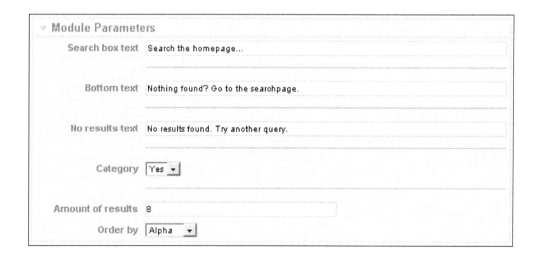

Most parameters are self-explanatory, but let's take a look at them:

- **Search box text** — here we will place the text that will appear in the search input box on the frontend.
- **Bottom text** — is a bit confusing, as it says "Nothing found?...". Well, in fact this has nothing to do with "No results found...". It only means that of all the results found, none match our needs. So we are allowed to go to the search page and see the full list of results, as the AJAX search serves us a limited list only.
- **No results text** — is what appears when nothing is found.
- **Category** — lets us decide if the category title is to be shown or not.
- **Amount of results** — relates to the limited list that we commented on before, and indicates the number of results that will be shown. If visitors find a useful link, they will click on it, and if not, they will be able to go to the full search page and see the full list.
- **Order by** — is the last parameter that gives us the possibility to select the ordering criteria. For now, we will use alphabetical ordering.

Don't forget to enable the module, and select **search** as its module position.

 It would also be a good idea to disable our previous **Basic Search** module.

If we refresh the frontend, we will see something similar to the following screenshot:

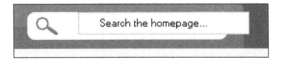

It's evident that we need to make some CSS adjustments, and it will be more evident when we try to perform a search. For example, on performing another "Lorem ipsum" search, we will see something like the next screenshot:

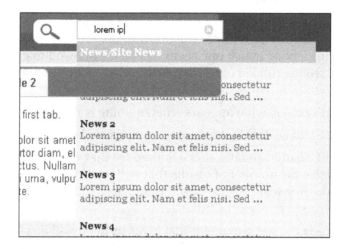

One of our previous modules – the tabs one – is appearing over our new module. This has to be a problem with CSS styles, most surely with the z-indexes. So we will need to search the problem, and try to correct it. It's time to do a little CSS magic! Look for the `modules/mod_ajaxsearch/css/search.css` file inside our Joomla! installation. Open it in your desired editor and look for the following piece of code:

```
#suggestions{
   width:290px;
   position: absolute;
   left: 0;
   top: 25px;
   display:none;
}
```

We will modify it a bit by adding a z-index clause as follows:

```
#suggestions{
   width:290px;
   position: absolute;
   left: 0;
   top: 25px;
   display:none;
   z-index: 5000;
}
```

That will solve the problem. However, as we are already here, we are going to make some more modifications. Search for the following code:

```
.ajaxsearch .inputbox {
  width: 156px;
  height:15px;
  padding: 3px 0 3px 20px;
  margin: 0;
  border: 1px solid #999999;
  font-size: 10px;
  background-image: url(modules/mod_ajaxsearch/img/search_loop.gif);
  background-repeat: no-repeat;
  background-position: 3px 5px;
  float: left;
}
```

We are going to change the border to 0px, add a negative margin on the left, add a top margin, and make it's width a bit smaller as follows:

```
.ajaxsearch .inputbox {
  width: 136px;
  height:15px;
  padding: 3px 0 3px 20px;
  margin: 0;
  margin-left: -20px;
  margin-top: 5px;
  border: 0px;
  font-size: 10px;
  background-image: url(modules/mod_ajaxsearch/img/search_loop.gif);
  background-repeat: no-repeat;
  background-position: 3px 5px;
  float: left;
}
```

Now only one small change remains to be made—the small closing image that appears to the right-hand side of the input box that is controlled by this code:

```
#loading-not{
    position: absolute;
    top: 6px;
    left: 155px;
```

We will change it to:

```
#loading-not{
    position: absolute;
    top: 6px;
    left: 135px;
```

With all those changes made our AJAX search will look similar to the following screenshot:

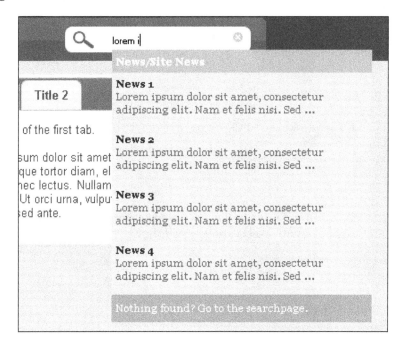

This time it looks much better and we are offering a nice feature to our site visitors, who will be able to find what they are looking for without the need to reload the page. Well, with that, we are done with our AJAX search feature.

If enabling this module seems to cause problems with other modules, it may again be that the module load of the jQuery library again interferes with that of the other modules' own loads. This module loads the jQuery library at the following line in the `modules\mod_ajaxsearch\mod_ajaxsearch.php` file:

```
$document->addscript(JURI::root(true).'modules'.
        DS.'mod_ajaxsearch'.DS.'js'.DS.'jquery-
        1.3.2.min.js');
```

Commenting this line will solve some problems, but then, what happens if no other library is loading the jQuery library? Our module won't work. How can we solve this problem? Keep reading and we will find a solution together.

To see this example, first we need to load a file from this module. The file is placed in `modules/mod_ajaxsearch` and is called `mod_ajaxsearch.php`. Open it in your desired editor and look for the following code:

```
$document->addscript(JURI::root(true).'modules'.
            DS.'mod_ajaxsearch'.DS.'js'.DS.'jquery-1.3.2.min.js');
$document->addscript(JURI::root(true).'modules'.
            DS.'mod_ajaxsearch'.DS.'js'.DS.'script.js');
```

As you can see in the module code, `$document->addscript` is being used to add scripts to our site header. So, first we need to know if jQuery is loaded in order to decide whether or not it should be loaded again. First, comment the previous lines and then look at the following code:

```
$custom  = '<script type="text/javascript">' ."\n";
$custom .= 'if (typeof jQuery == "undefined") {' ."\n";
$custom .= 'var script = document.createElement("script");' ."\n";
$custom .= 'script.setAttribute("type","text/javascript");' ."\n";
$custom .= 'script.setAttribute("src", "/modules/mod_ajaxsearch/js/
            jquery-1.3.2.min.js");' ."\n";
$custom .= 'document.getElementsByTagName("head")[0].
            appendChild(script);' ."\n";
$custom .= 'var script = document.createElement("script");' ."\n";
$custom .= 'script.setAttribute("type","text/javascript");' ."\n";
$custom .= 'script.setAttribute("src", "/modules/mod_ajaxsearch/js/
            script.js");' ."\n";
$custom .= 'document.getElementsByTagName("head")[0].
            appendChild(script);' ."\n";
$custom .= '}else{ ' ."\n";
$custom .= 'var script = document.createElement("script");' ."\n";
$custom .= 'script.setAttribute("type","text/javascript");' ."\n";

$custom .= 'script.setAttribute("src", "/modules/mod_ajaxsearch/js/
            script.js");' ."\n";
$custom .= 'document.getElementsByTagName("head")[0].
            appendChild(script);' ."\n";
$custom .= '}' ."\n";
$custom .= '</script>' ."\n";

$document->addCustomTag($custom);
```

First we will create a `$custom` variable and place some JavaScript code inside it. In the following code we are checking if jQuery is undefined:

```
$custom .= 'if (typeof jQuery == "undefined") {' ."\n";
```

If jQuery is undefined, it would mean that the jQuery library has not been loaded. So if we want to use it, we will need to load it as follows:

```
$custom .= 'var script = document.createElement("script");' ."\n";
$custom .= 'script.setAttribute("type","text/javascript");' ."\n";
$custom .= 'script.setAttribute("src", "/modules/mod_ajaxsearch/js/
           jquery-1.3.2.min.js");' ."\n";
$custom .= 'document.getElementsByTagName("head")[0].
           appendChild(script);' ."\n";
```

We create a `script` element and then we add a `type` attribute to it with the value `text/javascript`. In a similar fashion we add a `src` attribute, which has the path to the jQuery library as its value. Later we append it to the `head` section of our site. After this is done, we do the same for the module's own JavaScript code as follows:

```
$custom .= 'var script = document.createElement("script");' ."\n";
$custom .= 'script.setAttribute("type","text/javascript");' ."\n";
$custom .= 'script.setAttribute("src", "/modules/mod_ajaxsearch/js/
           script.js");' ."\n";
$custom .= 'document.getElementsByTagName("head")[0].
           appendChild(script);' ."\n";
```

The important part here comes in the following line:

```
$custom .= '}else{ ' ."\n";
```

If the jQuery library is loaded, the `else` part will be executed and only the module's own JavaScript code will be loaded:

```
$custom .= 'var script = document.createElement("script");' ."\n";
$custom .= 'script.setAttribute("type","text/javascript");' ."\n";
$custom .= 'script.setAttribute("src", "/modules/mod_ajaxsearch/js/
           script.js");' ."\n";
$custom .= 'document.getElementsByTagName("head")[0].
           appendChild(script);' ."\n";
```

Lastly, we need to put in the following line:

```
$document->addCustomTag($custom);
```

It works in a similar fashion to `$document->addscript`, but instead of creating a script tag, it will load our own code. And that's it, the module is now prepared to decide if it needs to load the jQuery library or not.

I've placed this code in a file called `ajax_search.txt` in the code bundle, so you don't need to write it all on your own.

Then, we need to make another tiny modification—I promise you this one is very tiny. Just open the file `modules/mod_ajaxsearch/js/script.js` and change the following line:

```
$(document).ready(function()
```

Modify it as follows:

```
jQuery(document).ready(function()
```

Also, change all the `$` in the document to `jQuery`. This last change is needed if you were previously using MooTools so that jQuery doesn't conflict with it. And that's all, but you can also check the other extensions.

Some other extensions to try

The following are some other interesting Joomla! extensions:

- **PixSearch Ajax Search module**—another interesting module that works mostly in the same way, just in case you want to check other options

- **RokAjaxSearch**—another interesting option, this extension works with the MooTools JavaScript library

Tips and tricks

I just want to make sure you don't miss these handy tips, and hope that they are useful to you:

- Our jTabs module can be mixed with the "Modules Anywhere" module to load modules into our tabs. This way you will have all the features of our tabs module, with the possibilities of loading the modules you want in the tabs. And if you also place the "Mini FrontPage" module in it we will end up with a very, very powerful mix of components.

- The Content Slider Module uses the jQuery tools library, which we can find here in `http://flowplayer.org/tools/`, and we can take advantage of this to modify the module. For example, if we want to add a nice, easing animation, we can modify the `modules/mod_slider/mod_slider.php` file. Search for the following code:

```
<script type="text/javascript" language="javascript">
(function($){
  $(document).ready(function(){
    $('div.csm_scrollable.<?php echo $uid; ?>').scrollable({
      size:1,
```

```
    }).autoscroll(<?php echo $interval; ?>);
  });
}) (jQuery);
</script>
```

Change it to:

```
<script type="text/javascript" language="javascript">

(function($){

  $(document).ready(function(){

    $.easing.custom = function (x, t, b, c, d) {
        var s = 1.70158;
        if ((t/=d/2) < 1) return c/2*(t*t*(((s*=(1.525))+1)*t -
            s)) + b;
        return c/2*((t-=2)*t*(((s*=(1.525))+1)*t + s) + 2) + b;
    }

    $('div.csm_scrollable.<?php echo $uid; ?>').scrollable({
      size:1,
      easing: 'custom',
      speed: 700,
      loop:true

    }).autoscroll(<?php echo $interval; ?>);

  });

}) (jQuery);

</script>
```

I've found this example on the http://flowplayer.org/tools/ site, you can find it under this link http://flowplayer.org/tools/demos/scrollable/easing.html.

If the previous method of detecting whether jQuery is loaded is not working for you, there's another interesting option. It consists of checking all of the modules we are using that make use, and load their own copy, of the jQuery library, and then commenting the lines of code that load the jQuery library. Just make sure that no module loads its own copy of the jQuery library, and then load only one copy of the jQuery library in the template, just before <jdoc:include type="head" />. In this way we will be sure that only one copy of the library is being used, and that it is loaded before all other libraries.

Summary

Well, we are at the end of the chapter, and we have seen quite a lot in it. We have put our content into tabs, created interesting article sliders, and added AJAX search capabilities to our site. These things alone can make a site look more interesting to our visitors and can also help us to show more content in the same available space.

We have also seen how to solve some problems in our modules and some tips at the end. I really hope this chapter has been interesting to you. Also, before going onto Chapter 3, why don't you try all these things on a demo site? It can be fun. I will be waiting for you in Chapter 3, don't be late! There are some interesting topics such as video plugins, audio and SWF files, and a lot more that await you.

3
Embedding Rich Media Features with Joomla! Plugins

"Small details make a big difference".

I've always believed that small details are what make sites look great. I think this is also true in the case of Joomla! plugins. Plugins are the smallest of extensions, but they give us great potential.

Plugins can also be useful for other less technical site administrators, who will find the code easier to write than the usual HTML code. There are lots of ways in which plugins can help make our site better, and in this chapter we are going to see some of them, such as:

- Concept of plugins—what they are and how they work
- A code highlighter plugin
- captbunzo's Flickr Album Plugin
- SC jQuery, a library loader plugin

I hope you will like this chapter. Let's get started.

Concept of plugin—what is a Joomla! plugin and how does it work?

As I have said previously, plugins are the smallest of Joomla! extensions and they work in a different way.

Components are placed usually in the central part of our site and are mostly used to display and organize our site content, such as articles, photo galleries, and even the products of a shop.

Modules tend to be smaller in complexity, work along components, and appear surrounding the central zone of our site.

Both these types of extensions show site visitors a wide variety of content, information, images, and so on.

Plugins work in a different fashion and, usually, more than displaying content, they are used to modify them. For this purpose, plugins are called in response to some Joomla! or user-defined events.

Joomla! events are a bit of a complex concept, but let's keep it simple. For example, displaying our content may seem like quite a simple task, but during that time some events are triggered. Among others we may find:

- `onPrepareContent` — when contents are being prepared
- `onBeforeDisplayContent` — just before contents are displayed
- `onAfterDisplayContent` — when our contents are displayed

Plugins can be defined to be executed when these events are triggered.

So, if we have a plugin that reads our content and finds a "www.something" text to create a link, we can define our plugin to be executed in the `onPrepareContent` event.

This way our content will be modified before being displayed. In an extremely basic way, it works, as shown in the following diagram:

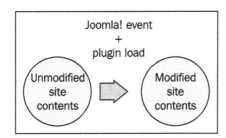

Well, it's pretty basic, but we are not going to enter into the "plugin development" garden. I just wanted to show you the basic way in which plugins work. Let's again take our previous example—the image gallery we created in Chapter 1. For our gallery to work, we wrote the following code in one of our articles:

```
{ppgallery}/stories/ppgallery{/ppgallery}
```

And when we enabled the plugin, instead of just showing the code in the frontend, a gallery was presented to us. If you check the source code of the page, you will see something like this:

```
<span style="color: #000000; font-family: Arial, Helvetica, sans-
serif; font-size: 11px; line-height: normal; -webkit-border-
horizontal-spacing: 2px; -webkit-border-vertical-spacing: 2px;"><span
class="pp_gallery">
<span class="ppg_thbox10"><span class="ppg_thb"><a href="/images//
stories/ppgallery/image_1.jpg" rel="prettyPhoto[pgg10]" title=""
target="_blank"><img src="/cache/images//stories/ppgallery/200x150_
q75_t_image_1.jpg" alt="image_1.jpg" width="200" height="150"
title="image_1.jpg" /></a></span></span>
   .
   .
   .
<span class="ppg_clr"></span>
```

So our simple line of code `{ppgallery}/stories/ppgallery{/ppgallery}` has been converted to a full and complex HTML code that is able to display our image gallery. When did this happen? Well, this time the change has been made on the `onPrepareContent` event, which happens when content is being prepared. The plugin detects our previous line of code and replaces it with all the HTML code required for the gallery.

 You can find a lot of information about Joomla! events and plugins at `http://docs.joomla.org/Tutorial:Plugins`.

With this knowledge, we can see how powerful Joomla! plugins can be. Not only do plugins help us enhance our content, but they are also a tool for less-technical people to introduce great-looking contents into their site with minimum knowledge.

Next, we are going to look at some interesting plugins.

Code highlighter plugin

Code highlighter extensions are very useful when creating tutorial sites, code blogs, and so on. The difference they can make is great and these plugins also turn some difficult-to-read code into great-looking code.

For this example, we are going to use a very interesting extension called **Core Design Chilicode plugin**. As always, we can search for it in the JED or else use the following URL:

`http://extensions.joomla.org/extensions/edition/code-display/7250.`

Download it, then go to our administrator panel, then to **Extensions | Install/Uninstall**, and install the downloaded file.

Before taking a look at the parameters of this extension (in fact, before we can use it), we need to install another extension, the **Core Design Scriptegrator plugin**, which can be found at:

`http://extensions.joomla.org/extensions/core-enhancements/scripts/3030.`

This plugin is used to load libraries, like jQuery itself, which are needed. These libraries are for the code highlighter extension. Why aren't these extensions placed in the code highlighter extension itself? Well, the developer, wisely I have to say, has decided to separate this library loader plugin. This has been done so that all of the other extensions from this developer can use these libraries without having to place them in every extension they create. It also saves the necessity for each extension to load a copy of the library.

As I've said, this is a wise way of doing things. Now enough talking, we will download and install that plugin. Go to **Extensions | Plugin Manager** and look for **System | Core Design Scriptegrator plugin**. Enable it and also open it to see its parameters:

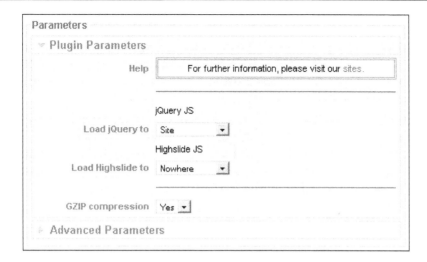

Very few parameters need to be changed, but we will take a look at them:

- **Load jQuery to** — is very self-explanatory; as this plugin is used to load libraries for all other plugins to use, the jQuery field was very expected. We can select from **Nowhere**, **Site**, **Administration** or **Both**. This time we only need the library to be loaded in the "site" or the "frontend".

- **Load Highslide to** — is used for other extensions from the developer. As this plugin doesn't need it, we can safely leave this as **Nowhere**.

- **GZIP compression** — is enabled by default, which is okay because it will make our libraries smaller and faster to download. Anyway, if we detect any problem, we can disable this.

Advanced parameters are about the Highslide library, so we don't need to take a look at them for now. We are ready to check the other plugin. Without leaving the **Plugin Manager** screen, look for **Core Design Chilicode plugin** and open it. The following screenshot shows the plugins admin screen:

Not many parameters here, just two of them:

- **Default language**—decides the default language to be used from a wide range of languages. As we can define this parameter later, we will leave it at **None**. But if you find yourself using a language more often than others, you could define it here—just to save some work later.

- **Default source**—here we can select **Content** or **File**. For our example, we are going to use **Content** as the plugin that will show the contents of one of our articles. In case we want to use **File**, we will need to define the folder where our files will be placed. This is done in the advanced parameters section, as we can see in the following screenshot:

The only parameter in the **Advanced Parameters** section is as follows:

- **Script directory**—if in the previous parameter we have selected to use **File** as the content source, here we will need to define where those files are placed. We can leave it as it is, as we are not going to use it.

Don't forget to enable both the plugins.

Now that we are done with the preparation, we can make use of this extension. But first we need an article where we can use it. I'm going to create a new section because as of now we only have one section called **News** and I wouldn't like to use it for this example. Navigate to **Content | Section Manager** and create a section called **Site content**.

We will also create a category called **Plugins** inside this section. Go to **Content | Article Manager** and create a new article. We are going to call this article **Code Highlighting**.

Now imagine we have the following content in our article:

```
Here we have some sample content for our article:

for($i=0; $i<250; $i++){
  echo "Keep reading";
}

And now some bit more:

<div id="header">
  <p>This is the header content</p>
</div>
```

In the next screenshot, we can see how it will more or less look on our frontend:

```
Code Highlighting
Here we have some sample content for our article:
for($i=0; $i<250; $i++){
echo "Keep reading";
}
And now some bit more:
<div id="header">
<p>This is the header content</p>
</div>
```

This will be very difficult to read. So we are going to enhance it a bit using our previously installed plugin. Go back to the **Article Manager** screen. In order to use the plugin, we will write something like:

```
{chilicode language source} content {/chilicode}
```

The parameters are:

- chilicode — is the plugin's "name" and won't change.
- language — indicates the language coloring that will be used. We can select from a wide range: JavaScript, PHP, MySQL, HTML, Java, C++, C#, Delphi, and LotusScript.
- source — can be either content or file. We are going to use content.

Let's modify our contents accordingly; they will look more or less as follows:

```
Here we have some sample content for our article:

{chilicode php content}

  for($i=0; $i<250; $i++){
      echo "Keep reading";
    }
{/chilicode}

And now some bit more:

{chilicode html content}

  <div id="header">
  <p>This is the header content</p>
  </div>

{/chilicode}
```

Check the following screenshot to see how these changes will affect the appearance of our article:

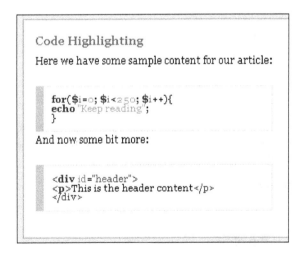

It's much better now. Our code samples look better and are a lot more readable (with very less effort required, and as we have commented before, in a very easy way).

Some other extensions to try

Of course, there are many other options. Some of them are as follows:

- **RJ_InsertCode**—supports other interesting languages such as XML, Python, Perl, Visual Basic, and many others. If you don't find the language you need in our previous sample, maybe this one has it included.

- **CodeCitation**—is a very interesting option, as it lets us define the tag that will encapsulate our code, hence making it easier to remember. It also supports some other interesting languages.

As always, we can find these extensions and many others by searching the JED.

captbunzo's Flickr Album plugin

Our next stop will be something very interesting that will add some quality content to our site—we are going to see a Flickr plugin. With this plugin, we will be able to insert Flickr galleries in our articles, helping us to add images that complement our articles.

Search for "captbunzo's Flickr Album Plugin" in the JED or use the following link:

```
http://extensions.joomla.org/extensions/external-contents/photo-
channels/6566.
```

You can use the method you prefer. Following the download link on the JED page will direct us to the author's page where we will be able to download the plugin.

There you will find two versions, one for PHP4 and the other for PHP5. Download the one that suits your needs.

After doing so, we will go to the admin screen, **Extensions | Install/Uninstall**, which will present us with the installation screen for extensions. Here we can search for our extension and click on the **Upload File & Install** button. If all goes as expected, the plugin will be installed without problems and we will be able to find it in **Extensions | Plugin Manager**.

Look for **Content - Flickr Album**; it will be disabled for now:

Clicking on the red cross will enable the plugin. We can do so now so that we don't forget about it. Our next step will be clicking on the plugin name so that we can access the plugin's admin screen. This screen will look similar to the following screenshot:

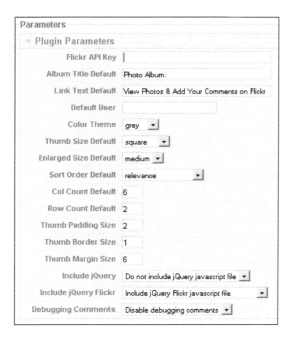

In this screen, we will be able to set up our options. Let's take a look at the parameters:

Parameter	Description
Flickr API Key	This is very important, as we will need an API key before using the plugin. However, it's quite easy to get an API key from the www.flickr.com page. Once you get your own API key, you need to place it here.
Album Title Default	This will be the default title that will appear over the image gallery. This title can be changed when invoking the gallery or later.
Link Text Default	This will generate a link to Flickr. We can place the text that will appear on the link.
Default User	Here we can indicate the default user from whom we will get the photos. We can follow the instructions from http://joomla.paulthompson.net/ to do so.
Color Theme	This is the first of the design parameters. Here we can select the color for the image border.
Thumb Size Default	Here, as the name implies, we can select the size of the images — **square** being the smaller one. We will be leaving this as is for now.

Parameter	Description
Enlarged Size Default	This time we can select the size of the enlarged or pop-up image—medium size will be okay for the images I will be using, but you can select any other size of your preference.
Sort Order Default	With this parameter, we will be able to select the ordering preferences for our images. As I've uploaded only a few images, this doesn't matter for me, but take a look at the options and select the one you prefer.
Col Count Default and **Row Count Default**	This will be used to select how many columns and rows will be presented with our gallery, directly affecting the number of images shown.
Thumb Padding Size and **Thumb Margin Size**	These options will affect the separation between images. Though we could change this in our CSS files, we can do so here for convenience. For now we will be leaving these parameters as they are.
Thumb Border Size	This is another similar parameter. We can select the border size for our images here. I think 1px will be enough for our border size.
Include jQuery	This is an important parameter that will let us decide whether we want to include the jQuery library or not. As we have already loaded this library for other extensions, here we will select to not include the library.
Include jQuery Flickr	This will include the Flickr jQuery plugin (as we need it in our example). We will leave this option as it is.
Debugging Comments	If something fails, we may use this option to try to find the problem. But for now, leave it at **Disable debugging comments**, as we don't want any message to be shown.

And that's all. We have finished configuring the plugin; now save the changes. Now to the interesting part—using the plugin. To use the plugin, we are going to create a new article, but you can use an existing one if you wish. Go to **Content | Article Manager** and create a new article.

I'm going to call this article **Flickr demo**, but this really doesn't matter. The important part will be the content for the article:

```
This is a demo of the flickr plugin:
{flickr-album}Type=User, User=46665027@N07{/tlickr-album}
In order to call the plugin we use the following tag:
{flickr-album}
Which we close using this one:
{/flickr-album}
```

Inside these two tags, we can specify some parameters in order to adapt the gallery to our needs. In the example, we are defining the `Type` as `User` and the user ID to be used. Those parameters and the ones configured in the plugin admin screen will result in a gallery similar to the following screenshot:

Sadly, I think I'm not such a good photographer. But, hopefully, this will serve as an example of what we can achieve with this plugin. Of course, we can specify some other parameters in the plugin call. We can see a full list at the following website:

`http://joomla.paulthompson.net/.`

Some of these include:

- `Title`—the title we want to use for our gallery
- `Type=Search`—to show photos from a search instead of a user
- `Keywords=world domination`—used with the previous parameter in order to perform the search

All of these options give us great configuration capabilities, which will allow us to use this plugin on lots of occasions to complement our articles with useful images.

Some other plugins to try

There are many other plugins that we can use in our site. Some of these are:

- **AutoFacebook plugin** — this plugin will put your Joomla! article's title into your Facebook status message and can be very useful to attract Facebook visitors to your site.

- **The Ultimate Social Bookmarking Plugin** — is an interesting plugin that will let our site visitors submit our articles to social networks, thus bringing more visitors to our site.

As always, we can find these extensions on the JED.

SC jQuery

For our third plugin, we are going to see something less visible. In the previous chapters, as well as in this chapter, we have seen modules and plugins that introduced into our site some very nice effects.

The **SC jQuery** plugin helps us with jQuery loading and has some nice features, even more than what you can see at first sight. Some of them, as said in the JED, are as follows:

- **Minified version of jQuery 1.3** — loads a "compressed" version of jQuery, saving us a bit of bandwidth

- **Executes noConflict() after jQuery has been loaded** — in order for other libraries to be used alongside jQuery, just like MooTools

- **jQuery UI integration and templates** — is a curious extra, but we will be able to decide whether to include it or not

- A place to add our own code to the template header

I'm going to leave the last and most interesting one untold, but we will see it later. Stay tuned so you don't miss it!

Well, now search for "SC jQuery" in the JED or load this URL: `http://extensions.joomla.org/extensions/core-enhancements/scripts/7230`. Once we are there, we will download the extension.

The next step is to install the file from our administrator screen **Extensions | Install/ Uninstall**. Once we have done so, we are ready to go. Under **Extensions | Plugin Manager**, we will be able to find our newly installed plugin. Just search for **System - SC jQuery** and locate the plugin.

Enable it from the manager screen and then click on it to see its details. The next screenshot is showing just that:

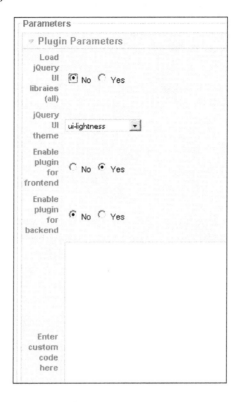

Though most of the parameters are self-explanatory, I would like to take a look at them with you:

- **Load jQuery UI libraries (all)** — I've set this to **No**, as only our tabs module uses the jQuery UI. If we don't modify its code (because it will continue to do so), it's of no use loading jQuery UI again.

- **jQuery UI theme** — this includes the images and the CSS style that make the jQuery UI themes, in the case of using the previous option: here we can decide the appearance.

- **Enable plugin for frontend** — this will load the plugin and thus the jQuery library in the frontend. I've selected **Yes**.

- **Enable plugin for backend** — we will be leaving this as **No** because we don't need it for now.

- **Enter custom code here** — lastly we are presented with a textarea that will let us introduce any code we want. Any code put here will be placed into a document-ready function.

And that's all. Just don't forget to enable the plugin. If all of this goes well, we won't see any differences in our frontend. However, if we check the source code of the template, we will see this:

```
<script type="text/javascript" src="/plugins/system/scjquery/js/
jquery-1.3.2.min.js"></script>

<script type="text/javascript" src="/plugins/system/scjquery/js/
jquery.no.conflict.js"></script>
```

These two lines of code will load the jQuery library and the "no conflict" script. Why don't you try the custom code parameter of the plugin? Just go back to the plugin admin screen and enter the following code in the custom code parameter field:

```
alert("Hello, How are you?");
```

Don't worry; we will remove this annoying message just after we try it!

Save the changes and go back to the frontend, reload, and that's it! We have just created an annoying message!

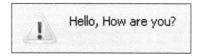

In fact, the ability to annoy visitors is not what I would like to show you; we will leave that for another chapter. At this point in time, I would like to show you the generated code.

On taking a look at the source code of our site, we will see some code as follows:

```
jQuery(function($){
  alert("Hello, How are you?");
});
```

As we can see, the code has been placed inside:

```
jQuery(function($){
```

And:

```
});
```

So our code will be able to work along with other libraries, such as MooTools. Before continuing, remove that code from the plugin.

And now we will see something very interesting and useful.

Along with all the functions we have seen, the SC jQuery plugin offers us a very useful extra feature. If we take a look at the plugin code, we see the following line of code at the end of it:

```
$app->set( 'jquery', true );
```

In newer versions of the plugin this line of code seems to have been removed. However we can modify the `plugins/system/scjquery.php` file and add that line to it, at the very bottom, just like this:

```
        . . .
        $app->set( 'jquery', true );
        $doc->setHeadData($headData);
        return true;
    }
}
```

This way we will be able to use the techniques we are about to show.

What's that? Well, the plugin is setting a variable called `jquery` with the value of `true`. How can we use this variable? Very easily; remember working with the AJAX search module in Chapter 2?

The fact that many modules were loading the jQuery library gave us some problems. In order to solve them, we needed to make a complex code similar to the following:

```
$custom  = '<script type="text/javascript">' ."\n";
$custom .= 'if (typeof jQuery == "undefined") {' ."\n";
$custom .= 'var script = document.createElement("script");' ."\n";
$custom .= 'script.setAttribute("type","text/javascript");' ."\n";
$custom .= 'script.setAttribute("src", "/modules/mod_ajaxsearch/js/
            jquery-1.3.2.min.js");' ."\n";
$custom .= 'document.getElementsByTagName("head")[0].
            appendChild(script);' ."\n";
$custom .= 'var script = document.createElement("script");' ."\n";
$custom .= 'script.setAttribute("type","text/javascript");' ."\n";
$custom .= 'script.setAttribute("src", "/modules/mod_ajaxsearch/js/
            script.js");' ."\n";
$custom .= 'document.getElementsByTagName("head")[0].
            appendChild(script);' ."\n";
$custom .= '}else{ ' ."\n";
```

```
$custom .= 'var script = document.createElement("script");' ."\n";
$custom .= 'script.setAttribute("type","text/javascript");' ."\n";
$custom .= 'script.setAttribute("src", "/modules/mod_ajaxsearch/js/
            script.js");' ."\n";
$custom .= 'document.getElementsByTagName("head")[0].
            appendChild(script);' ."\n";
$custom .= '}' ."\n";
$custom .= '</script>' ."\n";

$document->addCustomTag($custom);
```

In this code, we used JavaScript to detect if the jQuery library had been loaded, as follows:

```
if (typeof jQuery == "undefined") {
```

And, if it was not loaded, we loaded it. First we created a `script` element:

```
var script = document.createElement("script");
```

Then we added a `type` attribute to this `script` element:

```
script.setAttribute("type","text/javascript");
```

And, of course, we added a `src` attribute:

```
script.setAttribute("src", "/modules/mod_ajaxsearch/js/jquery-
1.3.2.min.js");
```

In the end, we added the following code to the head section of our site:

```
document.getElementsByTagName("head")[0].appendChild(script);
```

Now that the SC jQuery plugin is creating a variable, we can use just that in an easy way. Open the file `modules/mod_ajaxsearch/mod_ajaxsearch.php` and remove all the JavaScript. We will replace the JavaScript with this code:

```
$app =& JFactory::getApplication();

if(!$app->get('jquery') ){
  $document->addscript(JURI::root(true).'modules'.DS.
            'mod_ajaxsearch'.DS.'js'.DS.'jquery-1.3.2.min.js');
}
```

Here we are getting an instance of the application and trying to get the `jquery` variable that was defined earlier as follows:

```
$app->set( 'jquery', true );
```

Also uncomment the following line:

```
$document->addscript(JURI::root(true).'modules'.DS.
                'mod_ajaxsearch'.DS.'js'.DS.'script.js');
```

Looks easier, doesn't it? And it is more readable. We just check if the `jquery` variable is defined; if not, we load the jQuery library. If the variable returns `true`, it would mean that the plugin has already loaded the jQuery library. So we don't need to do it again and can follow with loading the module's own libraries.

Maybe you are thinking "Hey Jose, why didn't you show this first?" Well, I always like to see all the possible options. I feel the learning process is more complete if you are given all of the possible options.

The first solution was the one made by our own means, without the use of an external plugin. Now, with the introduction of another tool, we are able to upgrade the way in which we detect if the jQuery library has been loaded. And that's a good summary of a learning process, a continuous upgrade of knowledge.

Keep with us; we will see many other useful things!

Some other plugins to try

There are many other plugins just like the following plugin, but I just wanted to note this one in particular:

- **Google Ajax Library** — is a module that I think is interesting because it loads the library from Google, thus saving us a bit of bandwidth

Tips and tricks

This time it's more than a tip. I've one recommendation. As we have seen, the SC jQuery plugin enables us to detect whether the jQuery library has been loaded or not.

Though it may be a lot of work, I really think that in a real-world site, it would be useful to modify the plugins or modules we use to detect if jQuery has already been loaded, and then choose to load it or not in each case.

This way we can remove some conflicts between extensions and also save a huge load of bandwidth.

The problems are that if we install a newer version of those plugins or modules, our changes will be lost. But in any case, I think it's something to consider.

Also, by modifying the SC plugin to work as the Google Ajax, one can end up with less bandwidth being used.

Quite interesting!

Summary

Throughout this chapter, we have seen the basics of Joomla! plugins and also the very interesting SC jQuery plugin.

This plugin has let us detect if the jQuery library has already been loaded so that we can decide whether we need to load it again or not. But it will also help us more in the future because in the development chapters we will need the jQuery library to be loaded in the backend, and this extension does that.

Also, don't forget about the Flickr plugin that let us add useful images to our articles, making them even more interesting for our visitors.

I'm sure you can't wait to start with the development chapters, but we still have one chapter more about Joomla! modules. I just want to show you some modules that you can't miss, such as drop-down menus and many more.

Don't worry. We will be putting our hands to work sooner than you think!
Just keep reading!

4
One Last Look at Joomla! jQuery Modules

"Last but not least!"

This is the last chapter in which we are going to look at third party modules. After this we will start working on our own template modification, modules, and so on. Though I know that these are very interesting topics, I want to show you some things before I proceed. But don't worry, these will be interesting as well. In this chapter, we will see:

- The limitations of Joomla! menus
- How to create a drop-down menu with CSS alone
- jQuery powered Joomla! menu modules
- Creative ways of placing logging modules in our site

Interesting, isn't it? Let's start.

Limitations of Joomla! menu modules

By default, we have some interesting options when creating menus for our site — be it vertical menus or horizontal ones. This, mixed with the always useful CSS, will help us create very interesting menus for our site.

However, we face some limitations when working with menus, for example, drop-down menus. Though this can be achieved for sure, it's not as straightforward as we think it is. Take for example our template menu shown in the following screenshot:

It has worked for now. However, imagine that you want to convert the **News** menu into a drop-down menu, so that when a visitor moved his or her mouse pointer over it a structure like the following will be seen:

- News
    - News 1
    - News 2
    - News 3
    - News 4

First, we need to go to our administrator screen. For this example you can use any menu you want, but I am going to use the **Main Menu**.

Go to **Menus | Main Menu**; here you will see something similar to the following screenshot:

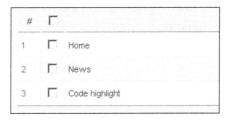

We only need to add some extra menu entries under the **News** menu. Click on **New | Articles | Article Layout**; in the screen that opens, near the top right-hand corner, you will see the **Parameters (Basic)** zone. Click on the **Select** button, and then select the **News 1** article, or any other article of your liking (as shown in the next screenshot):

Once you have this selected, you need to give the rest of the details (placed to the left-hand side), such as:

- **Title**—I'm going to enter **News 1**, but you can name it the way you want.
- **Alias**—again, I'm entering **News 1** here.
- **Link**—should be filled if you have selected the article.
- **Display in**—is where we can select in which menu this new menu entry will appear. The default **Main Menu** will work for us.
- **Parent Item**—is the important part; here you will choose under which option this new entry will appear. This time, it will be placed under the **News** menu.

After making these changes, you will see something similar to the following screenshot:

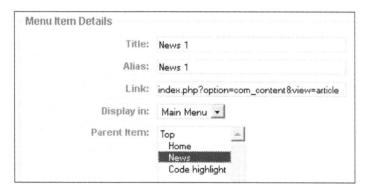

Repeat the process a few more times so that we have an interesting structure to work with. After all, we need some elements to put in our drop-down menu. When you have finished, and before going to the frontend to see the result of your work, you need to perform one little change in the **Main Menu** module.

In order to do this, we will go to the **Extensions | Module Manager** menu. Here, you will click on the **Main Menu** link. Check the **Parameters** zone; you need to modify the parameter as shown in the following screenshot:

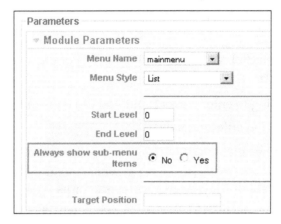

That's it, we need to change the **Always show sub-menu items** parameter to **Yes**. If you do so, in the frontend, you will see the sub-menu items. If we leave this parameter set to **No**, the sub-menu items will only appear if its menu item is selected. In your case that would be the **News** menu.

Let's take a look at the frontend:

Here we can see the result of our work. I've tried to highlight all of the menus so that you can see the effect. And because of the change we made in the module configuration, the submenus are shown even if we don't visit the **News** menu.

We are also seeing the limitations of our work. By default, Joomla! is not going to do anything else for us. So our work starts now.

Creating a drop-down menu with CSS alone

As we have seen in our previous image, for now, our menu is quite limited. The submenus are appearing just under their menus, but they don't really look quite good.

If we want to convert this unfinished menu into a working drop-down menu, we can use a lot of possibilities. We will be able to do it with CSS, a bit of JavaScript, or by using Joomla! extensions—and maybe I'm missing out some other way as well.

To start with, we are going to try it with CSS alone. Let's check the source code generated for our menu. It will look similar to the following:

```html
<div id="mainmenu">

  <ul class="menu">

    <li id="current" class="active item1">
    <a href="http://wayofthewebninja.com/"><span>Home</span></a></li>
    <li class="parent item2">
    <a href="/index.php?option=com_content&amp;view=category&amp;
      layout=blog&amp;id=1&amp;Itemid=2"><span>News</span></a>

    <ul>

      <li class="item4">
        <a href="/index.php?option=com_content&amp;view=article&amp;
          id=2&amp;Itemid=4"><span>News 1</span></a></li>

      <li class="item5">
        <a href="/index.php?option=com_content&amp;view=article&amp;
          id=3&amp;Itemid=5"><span>News 2</span></a></li>

      <li class="item6">
        <a href="/index.php?option=com_content&amp;view=article&amp;
          id=4&amp;Itemid=6"><span>News 3</span></a></li>

      <li class="item7">
        <a href="/index.php?option=com_content&amp;view=article&amp;
          id=7&amp;Itemid=7"><span>News 4</span></a></li>

    </ul>

    </li>

    <li class="item3">
      <a href="/index.php?option=com_content&amp;view=article&amp;
        id=9&amp;Itemid=3"><span>Code highlight</span></a></li>

  </ul>

</div><!-- End of mainmenu -->
```

Let's summarize this code so that we can see the important parts of it. Look closely:

```
<ul>
  <li>Menu 1
    <ul>
      <li>Submenu 1</li>
      <li>Submenu 2</li>
      <li>Submenu 3</li>
      <li>Submenu 4</li>
    </ul>
  </li>
</ul>
```

Now we can see the structure more easily, and we can also see that it includes an unordered list nested within another one. With this structure we are able to create a CSS drop-down menu with very little code.

Oh, I know I told you that we will start coding in the next chapter, but let's take this as a small introduction. Open the `templates/jj15/css/styles.css` file, and add the following code at the end:

```
/**
 * CSS dropdown styles
 */
ul.menu {
  padding: 0;
  margin: 0;
  list-style: none;
}

ul.menu li {
  float: left;
  position: relative;
}

ul.menu li ul {
  display: none;
  position: absolute;
  top: 25px;
  left: 0;
  z-index: 102;
}

ul.menu li ul li {
  background-color: #4C4841;
  padding: 4px;
```

```
    padding-left: 10px;
    width: 75px;
    border: 1px solid #5B5751;
}
ul.menu li:hover ul {
    display: block;
}
```

 You can find this code within the `css_dropdown_1.txt` file in the code bundle for Chapter 4 of the book.

Most of this code is only there to position the submenus under their menus, and also to give some color to the submenu elements. The important parts are as follows:

```
ul.menu li ul {
    display: none;
```

This code hides the submenu, so we can't see it. But then we have the following code:

```
ul.menu li:hover ul {
    display: block;
}
```

This code makes the menus visible when the mouse pointer is over the **Main Menu**. An image is better than a thousand words, so let's take a look at the result (as seen in the following screenshot):

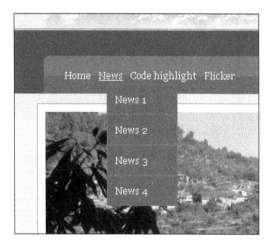

Why don't you try this out on your own?
This way you can see it in action.

Our menu now has a nice drop-down effect, and we have been able to accomplish it with only a bit of CSS. We can group our menus into drop-down menus to organize them better. But we have some limitations here:

- With the current code, we are able to nest only one sublevel. For example, if **News 2** has other menus inside, such as **News 2.1** and **News 2.2**, our CSS won't work for it.

- This code may not work in old browsers, such as IE 6, because it can't have the `:hover` pseudo class in elements other than links. As we have used it on a `li` element, it won't work.

All of these problems can be solved with some coding. For example, we can follow the guidelines found at the following links:

- `http://www.alistapart.com/articles/dropdowns/`
- `http://htmldog.com/articles/suckerfish/dropdowns/`

There's lot more out there. However, once we have seen an easy and fast way to have drop-down menus on standard compliant browsers, I think our next best step will be to use a Joomla! extension to create our menus.

jQuery-powered Joomla! menu modules

Using a Joomla! module for creating our menus has some benefits that must be taken into account. For example, they have some nice effects, such as fade effects, shadows, and many more.

These effects can make our site look a bit more appealing. They can also solve the problems that we have previously found, such as the menu not working in other browsers or the number of sublevels we are able to have.

With all this in mind we are going to see the **Superfish Dropdown Menu**. Search for it on the JED by that name, or find it at the following URL:

`http://extensions.joomla.org/extensions/structure-a-navigation/menu-systems/drop-a-tab-menus/6731`

As the module description itself states on this page, it's based on the Suckerfish-style menu – yes, the one we have been using in our CSS example – but this time with some jQuery added to it and all put into a Joomla! module.

Once we have downloaded it, our next step will be to go to the administrator screen of our site. Then go to **Extensions | Install/Uninstall**. Here, after selecting the file, click on the **Upload file & Install** button.

Hopefully, the extension will be installed without problems and you will find it in **Extensions | Module Manager**.

As this module will substitute our current **Main Menu** module, we need to disable the **Main Menu** module, and enable the **Superfish Menu** module as shown in the following screenshot:

After doing so, you can click on the **Superfish Menu**. Do so now, and look at the parameters found in it, as shown in the next screenshot:

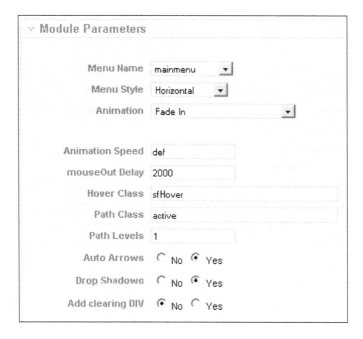

There are still more parameter's in the module, but we will start with the following ones:

- **Menu Name** — indicates the name of the menu to be used by the module. For now, we only have the **mainmenu**, so we have very little choice!

- **Menu Style** — provides quite a good range of options, such as **Horizontal**, **Vertical**, **Nav-Bar**, and **Accordion List**. For our example, we are going to need the **Horizontal** option.

- **Animation** — provides another good range of effects from slide to fade, or even both the effects together. This option doesn't really matter in our example, so choose any effect that you want.

- **Animation Speed** — is a parameter that will let us select the speed of the animation. This can be done by entering **slow**, **fast**, **def**, or the time in milliseconds in this field. For now, we will leave this parameter at its default value.

- **mouseOut Delay** — is an interesting parameter, which helps us define the time that elapses between the mouse leaving the menu, and the menu disappearing.

- **Hover Class** — is the CSS class that will be used when the mouse pointer is over the menu options.

- **Path Class** — is the CSS class that will be used for active elements in our menu.

- **Path Levels** — is the parameter that defines the number of menu levels that will remain active when we select the **Nav-Bar** style for our menu.

- **Auto Arrows** — will automatically add arrows to menus that contain submenus if we select **Yes**.

- **Drop Shadows** — is a nice effect that adds a good looking shadow to our menus; we will select **Yes**.

- **Add clearing DIV** — is used if you have been having problems with the menu — template problems I mean. Maybe it's because of the floating elements used with the menu; therefore, adding a clearing DIV may help. Our template doesn't have such problems, so we can leave this parameter set to **No**.

We have configured quite a few parameters, but before seeing our menu in action we need to do something more. At the very bottom of the parameters we can see the options for the jQuery library:

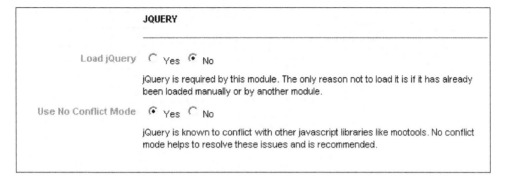

- **Load jQuery** — at this point in time we are already loading the jQuery library, so it's not necessary to load it again; select **No** here.

- **Use No Conflict Mode** — we can leave this option as **Yes** without problems.

We are almost done now, and only a few parameters need to be changed — the ones in the **Details** part, to the left-hand side — as we can see in the following screenshot:

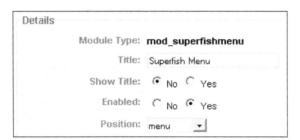

Here we need to perform some minor changes. The **Title** is not so important, as we are selecting **No** in **Show Title**. Of course, we need to enable the module if we haven't done so before. And last, but not least, is the module **Position**. For our current template and example, we are going to select the **menu** position of our template.

And that's all; we can save our changes and take a look at the frontend. If all has gone OK, and hopefully it has, we will be able to see something similar to the following screenshot:

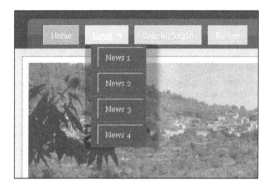

I know, I know, this needs some styling, but I just wanted you to see the result of our work. We can also comment on the benefits of this module over our previous CSS-only version. For example, and to name only some of them:

- It adds an arrow where submenus are present, so visually we know where more menus are expected to appear.

- The submenus don't disappear when the mouse pointer is not over them. Instead we can define for how much time the submenus will wait. This is especially useful for visitors with some difficulties.

- The effects, though not necessary, can make visiting our site more interesting.

Adapting the menu to suit our template

Now that we have our menu working, we are going to make the styling more in consonance with our template. Don't worry, this part will be easy, and more fun I think.

First open the `templates/jj15/css/styles.css` file and remove all of the styles that we placed before. These are all the styles that were placed under this comment:

```
/**
 * CSS dropdown styles
 */
```

This way we will start working from the ground up with our new styles. Now if we take a look at our source code, we can see a code similar to the following:

```html
<div id="mainmenu">

  <ul class="menu sf-menu sf-horizontal">

    <li id="current" class="first-child active item1"><a
      href="http://wayofthewebninja.com/"><span>Home</span></a></li>

    <li class="parent item2"><a
      href="/index.php?option=com_content&amp;view=category&amp;
      layout=blog&amp;id=1&amp;Itemid=2"><span>News</span></a>

      <ul>

        <li class="first-child item4"><a
          href="/index.php?option=com_content&amp;view=article&amp;
          id=2&amp;Itemid=4"><span>News 1</span></a></li>

        <li class="item5"><a
          href="/index.php?option=com_content&amp;view=article&amp;
          id=3&amp;Itemid=5"><span>News 2</span></a></li>

        <li class="item6"><a
          href="/index.php?option=com_content&amp;view=article&amp;
          id=4&amp;Itemid=6"><span>News 3</span></a></li>

        <li class="last-child item7"><a
          href="/index.php?option=com_content&amp;view=article&amp;
          id=7&amp;Itemid=7"><span>News 4</span></a></li>

      </ul>

    </li>

    <li class="item3"><a
      href="/index.php?option=com_content&amp;view=article&amp;
      id=9&amp;Itemid=3"><span>Code highlight</span></a></li>

    <li class="last-child item8"><a
      href="/index.php?option=com_content&amp;view=article&amp;
      id=10&amp;Itemid=8"><span>Flicker</span></a></li>

  </ul>

</div><!-- End of mainmenu -->
```

As we can see, it's mostly the same code that we have before installing the menu module. We have the two nested lists. However, some classes have been added, and this is great because this gives us more control when styling.

Note that some of these styles make mention of child elements, such as first-child, last-child, and so on. Child elements are elements that are inside another element. So the first-child would be the first element found inside the other element and the last-child would be the last.

This differentiation makes it easier to style elements; we can take advantage of these new classes.

But first, let's return to our administrator screen. Go to **Extensions | Module Manager**, and click on the **Superfish Menu**. We need to add something to the module parameters. Once in the module's admin screen, look for the **Custom Styling** parameter. It looks similar to the following screenshot:

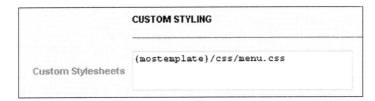

This parameter lets us add our custom CSS stylesheet. This way we don't need to modify module files, and we can create our own file. This file will prevail upon the module CSS files. For example, I've put in the following parameter:

```
{mostemplate}/css/menu.css
```

First save this change. Then we need to create the menu.css file in templates/jj15/css. Create the file and open it; we are going to add the following styles to it:

```
.menu{
  margin-top: -3px;
  margin-left: -15px;
}
```

This is only to move the menu a bit. Now add the background colors, borders, and so on, of the first-level li elements:

```
.menu li{
  background-color: #938F89;
  border: 1px solid  #211F1B;
}

.menu li a{
  border-top: 1px solid #DEDEDE;
  border-left: 1px solid #DEDEDE;
}
```

For the second-level `li` elements add the following styles:

```
.menu li ul li{
  background-color: #938F89;
  border: 1px solid  #211F1B;
}

.menu ul li li a{
  border-top: 1px solid #DEDEDE;
  border-left: 1px solid #DEDEDE;
}
```

For the current active menu add the following styles:

```
#current a{
  background-color: #9A0000;
  color: #ffffff;
  font-weight: bold;
  border-top: 1px solid #D70000;
  border-left: 1px solid #D70000;
}
```

And lastly, for the hovering elements add the following styles:

```
.sf-menu a:focus,  .sf-menu a:hover,  .sf-menu a:active {
  background:    #000000;
}
```

With all these changes, our menu will look more or less as follows:

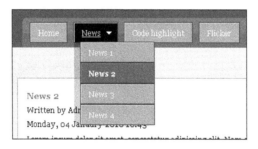

Much better now, isn't it? With very little effort our menu looks a lot better. Of course, this module has many other options, so why don't you give it a try? This is an extension that we could always use to modify and try out options, or to just play with it!

You can find the code for this example inside the `css_dropdown_2.txt` file in the code bundle for Chapter 4 of the book.

Some more extensions to try

Though this menu module can be a great solution for our site, there are also some other great extensions that we can use in other projects. We can find them by searching the JED:

- **FishEye Menu For Joomla 1.5** — generates icon menus. When you hover the mouse pointer over the elements, the icons get bigger. I think this can be quite useful in some templates.
- **HxD MooMenu** — is similar, in concept, to the module that we have been using. However, it uses MooTools instead of jQuery — it's just a question of personal taste.

Creative ways of placing login modules in our site

Most of the time we place login modules on our home page, where people can see them. This is OK, but what about the rest of the pages of our site? Maybe we don't need to have the login form in all of the pages on our site as it takes up space that can be used for other interesting things.

Then what can we do? It would be nice to have a small button that, when pressed, shows us the login form.

That's just what we are going to create next. We will use the **c7DialogMOD Module**. This module allows us to show another module inside a dialog box.

So why don't we explore this module as we always do? First, search for "c7DialogMOD Module" in the JED or use the following link:

```
http://extensions.joomla.org/extensions/style-a-design/popups-a-
iframes/9173
```

Download the module and install it. Go to **Extensions | Module Manager**. But before going into the newly installed module, we have something to do.

On the **Module Manager** screen click on the **New** button. Here we are going to create a new **Login** form:

We are going to call it "Login form", just to be a bit creative. Also, we don't need to enable the module, so we can keep it disabled. Save it, and now to the interesting part. Once you are back on the **Module Manager** screen, look for **c7dialogmod**, and click on it.

This will open the module's admin screen. Let's take a look at the following screenshot:

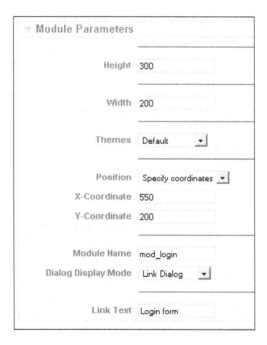

Most of these parameters are quite easy to configure. Well, in fact, all of them are easy to configure, but anyway, why don't we spend a few minutes going through them?

- **Hcight** — will be the height of our dialog box. For this example, I think **300** px will be OK. But we can change this later anyway.

- **Width** — works mostly as the previous one, but for the width instead of the height.

- **Themes** — as this module uses the jQuery UI themes, it comes with a selection of themes; here we can select the one we want. This really doesn't affect the result, so I will be leaving the default one. Just choose your favorite.

- **Position** — specifies where our dialog will appear. I think **Center** is a good place, as it puts the dialog in the very center of our screen.

- **X-coordinate / Y-coordinate** — is used along with the previous parameter set to specify coordinates; these two parameters define where we want the dialog to be placed.

- **Module Name** — is the parameter that specifies the module that we want to be loaded into the dialog. We are going to use **mod_login** for this example, so enter that here.

- **Dialog Display Mode** — has the two options: **Default Dialog** and **Link Dialog**. **Default Dialog** will load the dialog automatically when the page is loaded, and the **Link Dialog** will need a click on a button to open the dialog screen. **Link Dialog** will be the one for our example.

- **Link text** — is the text that will appear on the button commented previously. "Login form" or any text that you want can be used.

Just don't forget to enable the module. But in which position are we going to place it? There's no position defined yet. Therefore, we are going to create one. But this is going to be extremely easy, just open the `templates/jj15/index.php` file.

Once there, look for the following:

```
<div id="header">
```

Add the following code snippet just below that:

```
<div id="login">
  <jdoc:include type="modules" name="login" />
</div>
```

We are done with the `index.php` file. The next stop is the `templates/jj15/templateDetails.xml` file. Here we need to find the following code:

```
<positions>
```

Add a new module position, so we can use it later. For example, add the following code, (only the highlighted part):

```
        .
        .

        .
    <position>login</position>
</positions>
```

We are almost done. Only some minor CSS modifications are needed; open the
`templates/jj15/css/styles.css` file and search for the following code:

```
#header{
   height: 58px;
}
```

Modify it as follows:

```
#header{
   height: 58px;
   position: relative;
}
```

Add the following code below it:

```
#login{
   position: absolute;
   right: 0;
   z-index: 1;
}
```

Go to the administrator screen, then to **Extensions | Module Manager**, and open the
c7dialogmod module. We are going to configure some more details of the module, as
shown in the following screenshot:

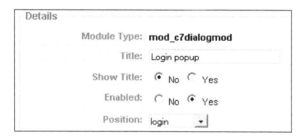

Here we need to check two things. First, we need to check if the module is **Enabled**,
and next, the **Position**. Next we are going to select our newly created position, that
is, **login**. We are done now, so let's save the settings and go to the frontend of
our site.

It's possible that in our frontend you will see something similar to the following screenshot:

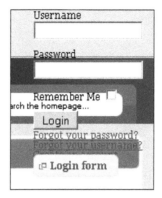

This means that we are having some JavaScript problems. But don't worry, we are here to learn how to solve such problems.

When working with different extensions, each extension makes use of the same or different JavaScript libraries and it's very hard not to come upon errors.

This time, as on other occasions, the problem we are facing is that our module is trying to load the jQuery library again. This is, therefore, conflicting with other modules that have already loaded the library.

But this problem is easy to solve—we have already done that in the past with the help of the SC jQuery plugin and the parameter this plugin sets. We will now put our hands to work; open the `modules/mod_c7dialogmod/mod_c7dialogmod.php` file. In this file we are going to search for a line similar to the following:

```
$document->addScript($burl.'modules/mod_c7dialogmod/jquery
            /jquery-1.3.2.js');
```

Here the module is loading the jQuery library, but, as this has already been done, problems arise. So how do we solve this? Modify the previous line to:

```
$app =& Jfactory::getApplication();

if( !$app->get('jquery') ){
  $document->addScript($burl.'modules/mod_c7dialogmod
            /jquery/jquery-1.3.2.js');
}
```

With two easy steps we have solved our problem; first we create an instance of getApplication and then use the get method to check if the jquery variable is set. If this parameter doesn't exist, we will load the jQuery library, if not, we don't.

After we have done so, we may find another error, depending on the module version. If you are using the same version as me, Firebug will display something like this:

Remember the admin zone of the c7dialogmod module? There we defined the module **Position** parameter, and as we wanted the module to appear centered, we selected **Center** in that parameter.

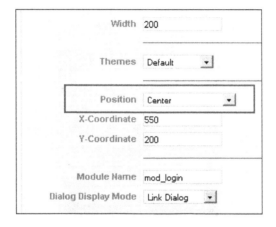

Let's work to solve this. Open the modules/mod_c7dialogmod/tmpl/default.php file and search for the following code:

```
$("#c7dialogmod").dialog({ autoOpen: false, position:<?php echo
$c7dialogmod_position ?>, height:<?php echo $c7dialogmod_height ?>,
width:<?php echo c7dialogmod_width ?>});
```

Here we need to change two things, so this line will be changed to the following:

```
$("#c7dialogmod").dialog({ autoOpen: false, position:'<?php echo
$c7dialogmod_position ?>', height:<?php echo $c7dialogmod_height ?>,
width:<?php echo $c7dialogmod_width ?>});
```

We have only added the quotes around `<?php echo $c7dialogmod_position ?>`, as the position needs to be quoted when making the dialog call. Also, we have added a `$` to the `c7dialogmod_width` variable. And that's it, now our module will work. Our login button will look as follows:

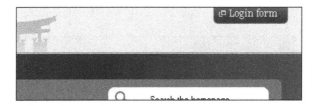

If we click on the button, we will see the following dialog, containing our login module:

Nice isn't it? This way we can have our login module accessible all over our site without taking the space required for other things.

This is one of those extensions that help us in making our site look better and also be useful at the same time. Throughout the next chapters, we will be creating extensions just like this one—useful and good looking.

Some other extensions to try

Of course, there are many other extensions we could be using, and searching the JED we can come across the following extensions:

- **R3D Floater**—similar to the one we have been using. It can show modules in a pop up that will slide from the left-hand side of our screen, disappearing moments later.

- **Ninja Shadow Panel**—another similar extension (commercial this time). Just search for it in the JED and take a look at it.

However, there are many other extensions. Just visit the JED and you will find lots of useful extensions.

Tips and tricks

The c7DialogMOD module can be used in some quite creative ways. For example, it can be used to show the login module on the home page, in a module position, and on the rest of the site it will show the dialog button that will open the dialog with the login module.

This way, visitors will see the full login form on the home page, but only the button on other pages, saving us some nice space.

Summary

This has been a very busy chapter. Though we have seen only two extensions, they have made our site look a lot better. At first we created a drop-down menu, allowing us to have lots of organized menus without using a lot of space.

We have done it using only CSS, and after using a Joomla! extension. After that we saw how to place a login module into a dialog box.

This time we placed the login module, but we could have placed any other module in the same way.

Also, we needed to solve some problems. As in real life scenarios, problems appeared when developing our demo site, but we have been able to solve these problems, and have understood the bigger problem behind it.

The next chapter will be full of useful things. So come on! Continue reading!

5
Refactoring Our Site

"Welcome to the code!"

Now, before continuing, we will try to refactor our site a bit. This is going to be a small chapter, where we will take a look at our site, modify it, and learn a bit more about how it works.

But what is all this refactoring about? Well, Wikipedia (`http://en.wikipedia.org/wiki/Code_refactoring`) says:

> *"Code refactoring is the process of changing a computer program's source code without modifying its external functional behavior in order to improve some of the nonfunctional attributes of the software. Advantages include improved code readability and reduced complexity to improve the maintainability of the source code, as well as a more expressive internal architecture or object model to improve extensibility."*

So that's what we are going to do, try to make our code better without changing how our site looks. At this moment we are using quite a good number of third-party extensions in our site. We all must agree that the creators of these extensions have done a great job, and that all of these extensions have helped us in preparing a great site.

However, we have a little problem here; each one of these extensions is loading their required libraries. In most cases these include the jQuery library.

It's necessary to load these libraries, as the creators behind these extensions don't know if the required libraries will be present on our site.

But we know that the necessary jQuery library is already present, so what's the point of loading it more than once?

This chapter is about those small things that visitors don't see, but that are necessary to make a well-developed site. Just follow along with me in this chapter. We are going to see:

- How to remove unnecessary jQuery loads
- What happens with jQuery UI
- Tips and tricks
- Some warnings

 Though you can pass over this chapter, and go directly to *Chapter 6, Getting Our Hands on Coding JavaScript*, I really encourage you to continue and learn the inner workings of our site. This knowledge will surely help you when developing any site.

Warning

In this chapter, we are going to do lots of modifications to our site, but some things have to be taken into account before making these changes.

The first thing that you should always do before making any changes is take a backup of your site. You can do this manually or by using an extension like Akeeba backup, which can be found in the JED or at the following link:

`http://extensions.joomla.org/extensions/access-a-security/backup/1606`

Having a backup copy is essential to restore a working copy of our site if a mistake is made.

Also, you may be wondering whether, later, if you install a newer version of the extension, you may lose all of the changes made. This can happen; therefore, we have made these modifications after we have finished installing the extensions we need.

But don't worry too much about that. You won't be installing a newer version of an extension every day. Mostly, you will install a newer version of the extension if bugs have been found or if the version introduces some features you want.

Otherwise, if the site is working nicely and there are no bugs or newer features, we don't need to update these extensions.

Anyway, the most important thing to remember is to backup. Always keep a backup of your work.

Removing unnecessary jQuery loads

As I have said, each one of the extensions that we are using is loading its own jQuery library, and thus makes our site needlessly load the library many times.

This makes our site download more files than are really necessary. Just take a look at the source code of your site. In the head section we can see the `script` tags that are loading the required libraries:

```
<script type="text/javascript"
    src="/plugins/system/cdscriptegrator/libraries/jquery
    /js/jsloader.php?files[]=jquery-latest.packed.js&amp;files[]=
    jquery-noconflict.js"></script>

  <script type="text/javascript"
    src="/plugins/system/cdscriptegrator/libraries/jquery/
        js/ui/jsloader.php?file=ui.core"></script>

  <script type="text/javascript"
    src="/plugins/system/scjquery/js/jquery-1.3.2.min.js"></script>

  <script type="text/javascript"
    src="/plugins/system/scjquery/js/jquery.no.conflict.js"></script>

  <script type="text/javascript"
    src="/plugins/system/scjquery/js/
        jquery-ui-1.7.2.custom.min.js"></script>

  <script type="text/javascript"
    src="/media/system/js/mootools.js"></script>

  <script type="text/javascript"
    src="/media/system/js/caption.js"></script>

  <script type="text/javascript"
    src="/plugins/content/ppgallery/res/jquery.js"
    charset="utf-8"></script>

  <script type="text/javascript"
    src="/plugins/content/ppgallery/res/jquery.prettyPhoto.js"
    charset="utf-8"></script>

  <script type="text/javascript"
    src="http://wayofthewebninja.com/modules/
        mod_ninja_shadowbox/ninja_shadowbox/js/adapter/
        shadowbox-jquery.js"></script>
```

```
<script type="text/javascript"
  src="http://wayofthewebninja.com/modules/
    mod_ninja_shadowbox/ninja_shadowbox/js/shadowbox.js"></script>

<script type="text/javascript"
  src="/modules/mod_ajaxsearch/js/script.js"></script>


<script type="text/javascript"
  src="http://wayofthewebninja.com/modules/
    mod_superfishmenu/tmpl/js/jquery.event.hover.js"></script>

<script type="text/javascript"
  src="http://wayofthewebninja.com/modules/
    mod_superfishmenu/tmpl/js/superfish.js"></script>

<script type="text/javascript"
  src="http://wayofthewebninja.com/modules/
    mod_c7dialogmod/jquery/ui.core.js"></script>

<script type="text/javascript"
  src="http://wayofthewebninja.com/modules/
    mod_c7dialogmod/jquery/ui.dialog.js"></script>

<script type="text/javascript"
  src="http://wayofthewebninja.com/modules/
    mod_c7dialogmod/jquery/ui.draggable.js"></script>

<script type="text/javascript"
  src="http://wayofthewebninja.com/modules/
    mod_c7dialogmod/jquery/ui.resizable.js"></script>
```

Here we can see that lots of JavaScript files are being loaded, and some of them are repeated. Surely, that doesn't make our site load faster.

Let's try to improve this as much as we can. Remember what we did in the previous chapters? We used the SC jQuery plugin in order to load the jQuery library. With the help of a variable created by this library we could also determine if the jQuery library needs to be loaded or not.

How was this done? If we open the `plugins/system/scjquery.php` file, at the very bottom of the file you can see the following code:

```
$app->set( 'jquery', true );
```

In newer versions of the plugin this line of code seems to have been removed. However we can modify the `plugins/system/scjquery.php` file and add that line to it, at the very bottom, just like this:

```
. . .
$app->set( 'jquery', true );
$doc->setHeadData($headData);
return true;
    }
  }
```

This way we will be able to use the techniques we are about to show.

This will set a variable `jquery` with the value `true`. Our next step is to use this variable to our benefit, just like we did in the **ajaxSearch** module. Open the `modules/mod_ajaxsearch/mod_ajaxsearch.php` file. We modified this file and it now appears as follows:

```
$app =& JFactory::getApplication();

if( !$app->get('jquery') ){
   $document->addscript(JURI::root(true).'modules'.DS.
                'mod_ajaxsearch'.DS.'js'.DS.'jquery-1.3.2.min.js');
}
```

First we need to get an instance of the global application object. We will then use the `get` method to try and read the `'jquery'` variable. If this variable doesn't exist, it would mean that the SC jQuery plugin has not been loaded, and thus the jQuery library won't be present.

If this happens, we will let the module load its own copy of the library. As we have seen in the previous chapters, this has helped us in reducing the number of times the library has been loaded.

Now we are going to look into the other extensions that we used, seeing how we can solve each situation.

Code highlight

Remember the Core Design Chili Code plugin extension? We used it to reformat some code, as we can see in the next image:

Code Highlighting

Here we have some sample content for our article:

```
for($i=0; $i<250; $i++){
echo 'Keep reading';
}
```

And now some bit more:

This plugin required the jQuery library, but as the plugin itself doesn't have the library included, another plugin from the same developers was needed—the Core Design Scriptegrator plugin. You can check it in **Extensions | Plugin Manager**:

System - Core Design Scriptegrator plugin

This plugins works much like the SC jQuery plugin, but for the extensions of the Core Design Chili Code plugin developers. This plugin loads the jQuery library, and some others that we don't need, in order for the other extensions to use it.

As we are using the SC jQuery plugin, we can disable the Scriptegrator plugin:

System - Core Design Scriptegrator plugin

But hey, then the **Core Design Chili Code** plugin stops working. Why? We have said that the Chili Code plugin needs the jQuery library, but we are using the SC jQuery plugin to provide it. At this point we need to check the Chili Code plugin source code, so just open `plugins/content/cdchilicode.php`. Here we can see the following piece of code:

```
// define language
if (!defined('_JSCRIPTEGRATOR'))
{
    Error::raiseNotice('',
            JText::_('CHILICODE_ENABLE_SCRIPTEGRATOR'));
    return;
}

// require Scriptegrator version 1.3.4 or higher
```

```
$version = '1.3.4';
if (!JScriptegrator::versionRequire($version))
{
 JError::raiseNotice('',
        JText::sprintf('CHILICODE_SCRIPTEGRATOR_REQUIREVERSION',
        $version));
   return;
}


if (!JScriptegrator::checkLibrary('jquery', 'site'))
{
   JError::raiseNotice('', JText::_('CHILICODE_MISSING_JQUERY'));
    return;
}
```

What does all this code do? It checks for the Core Design Scriptegrator plugin. If it doesn't find any evidence of the plugin, it raises some errors and returns.

We know that jQuery will be loaded. So we can comment the code mentioned, and the Chili Code plugin will work again.

That's it; we have just reduced one jQuery library load; ready for the next one?

pPGallery plugin

Remember our gallery plugin? Surely you do; we used it to create an interesting image gallery in our home page:

This is our next objective. This plugin also uses the jQuery library, as we can see by checking the source code of our site:

```
<script type="text/javascript"
    src="/plugins/content/ppgallery/res/jquery.js"
    charset="utf-8"></script>
<script type="text/javascript"
    src="/plugins/content/ppgallery/res/jquery.prettyPhoto.js"
    charset="utf-8"></script>
```

The prettyPhoto library will be loaded as required, but loading the jQuery library needs some work. This time we will be working with the `plugins/content/ppgallery.php` file. Here we need to find the following line:

```
$doc->addScript($relpath.'/plugins/content/ppgallery/res
        /jquery.js" charset="utf-8');
```

As we can see, this is where the plugin loads the jQuery library. We will modify this line to:

```
$app =& JFactory::getApplication();
if( !$app->get('jquery') ){
    $doc->addScript($relpath.'/plugins/content/ppgallery/res
            /jquery.js" charset="utf-8');
}
```

As in the previous instances, we use the variable set by the SC jQuery plugin to decide whether the jQuery library needs to be loaded or not.

Once we have done so, the pPgallery plugin won't load the jQuery library if it is present, thus saving us another load. We are almost done now, just keep up the good work.

Shadowbox

This time we need to think twice about this extension. Looking at the source code of our site we see the following:

```
<script type="text/javascript"
  src="http://wayofthewebninja.com/modules/mod_ninja_shadowbox/
        ninja_shadowbox/js/adapter/shadowbox-jquery.js"></script>
<script type="text/javascript"
  src="http://wayofthewebninja.com/modules/mod_ninja_shadowbox/
        ninja_shadowbox/js/shadowbox.js"></script>
```

We can see two library loads here:

- `shadowbox-jquery.js`
- `shadowbox.js`

However, though we may think the first one is a jQuery instance, it isn't. Does this mean we weren't using jQuery for this library? Not exactly; go to the administrator screen, then to **Extensions | Module Manager | Ninja Shadowbox.** There look for the **Parameters** zone; it will be more or less as follows:

Here we can see that when we first used the library we decided not to include the core JavaScript library. If we had included it, our source code would look as follows:

```
<script type="text/javascript"
  src="http://wayofthewebninja.com/modules/mod_ninja_shadowbox/
      ninja_shadowbox/js/lib/jquery.js"></script>

<script type="text/javascript"
  src="http://wayofthewebninja.com/modules/mod_ninja_shadowbox/
      ninja_shadowbox/js/adapter/shadowbox-jquery.js"></script>

<script type="text/javascript"
  src="http://wayofthewebninja.com/modules/mod_ninja_shadowbox/
      ninja_shadowbox/js/shadowbox.js"></script>
```

Here we can now see how the jQuery library is being loaded. This way, by selecting **Don't Include** in the module's parameters, our work will be done with this library.

 But we will need the SC jQuery plugin or to load the jQuery library ourselves.

This extension has been easy, as it includes a parameter that lets us select whether we want to load the jQuery library or not. But don't worry; only some extensions are left, and before we finish off the chapter we will see some very interesting things, just keep up with us!

AJAX Header Rotator

This was one of the first extensions we used, and is one of the most visible parts of our site. Do you remember it? Look at the following screenshot:

This extension works a bit differently than the others that we have seen. As you may have noticed, we haven't seen its library load on the header section of our site. That's because this library loads its necessary libraries within the body part of our site.

Why don't we look at this more closely? Open the modules/mod_jw_ajaxhr/mod_ jw_ajaxhr.php file, and search for the following code:

```
<script type="text/javascript"
    src="modules/mod_jw_ajaxhr/jquery.js"></script>

<script type="text/javascript">jQuery.noConflict();</script>

<script type="text/javascript"
    src="modules/mod_jw_ajaxhr/jquery.innerfade.js"></script>
```

In this way scripts are included just in the body section of our site. In the previous extensions we saw the following code:

```
$document->addscript
```

This code snippet added scripts to the head section of our site.

Does this change the way in which we can detect if the jQuery library has been loaded? No, we can detect it the same way as we have done before, as follows:

```
<?php
  $app =& JFactory::getApplication();
  if( !$app->get('jquery') ){
?>
```

```
<script type="text/javascript"
    src="modules/mod_jw_ajaxhr/jquery.js"></script>

<script type="text/javascript">jQuery.noConflict();</script>

<?php
    }
?>

<script type="text/javascript"
    src="modules/mod_jw_ajaxhr/jquery.innerfade.js"></script>
```

Done, just as we have been doing previously. Easy, isn't it?

Content Slider module

This is another of the easy ones, as there's a parameter in the module's admin screen that lets us define if we want to load, or not load, the jQuery library.

Just go to the administrator screen of our site, then go to **Extensions | Module Manager | Content Slider Module.** Look for the **Assume jQuery already loaded** parameter, as seen in the following screenshot:

When we worked with this extension we set the parameter to **Yes**, as we knew we had already loaded jQuery. We will keep this parameter set to **Yes**, just so that we don't unnecessarily load another jQuery library. The next two extensions will be a bit different, but keep reading!

What happens with jQuery UI

Through the last few pages we have accomplished our main objective: reducing the number of times our site loads the jQuery library. However, two extensions are left:

- The jQuery tabs module
- The c7DialogMOD module we used for our login form

These two extensions not only use the jQuery library, but also the jQuery UI library.

If you want to know more about jQuery UI visit `http://jqueryui.com/`. This is an interesting library that won't disappoint you. It is very useful.

The jQuery UI is a must for these two extensions, as is the library that provides the dialog and tabs methods. The problem here is that each one of these extensions loads its own copy of the UI library, and also a copy of the jQuery library.

This too is something that we can solve. Remember the SC jQuery plugin? It will also help us this time; just open it to take a look. Go to the administrator screen of our site and then go to **Extensions | Plugin Manager | System - SC jQuery**. Take a look at the **Parameters** zone. I have detailed the important part in the next image:

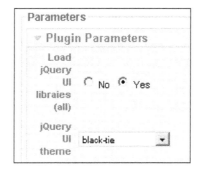

In these parameters we can not only select to load the jQuery UI library, but we can also decide which theme to use.

 Notice here that the plugin loads all of the jQuery UI libraries.

This will help us make all the extensions of our site share the same theme, and of course use the same library. If we don't do this, each library will try to use its own theme or library, which can therefore make our site look less attractive.

Usually, keeping color consistency makes the sites look better and more professional. Color consistency is an important part of every design. Some clients don't share this opinion, and prefer to have the largest variety of colors on their sites. Though this can be done, we will try to keep color consistency in our site, much to the delight of our site visitors.

We will now start working with these extensions. Next, we will see the c7DialogMOD extension.

c7DialogMOD

This was one of the last extensions we introduced. We used it to display a module in a dialog. The login module was selected, as shown in the following screenshot:

Changes needed in this extension will also be easy. All modifications will be made to the `modules/mod_c7dialogmod/mod_c7dialogmod.php` file. In this file, look for the following code:

```
switch ($c7dialogmod_theme){
  case lightness:
        $document->addStyleSheet($burl.'modules/mod_c7dialogmod
                    /jquery/theme/theme_lightness/ui.all.css');
          break;
  case darkness:
        $document->addStyleSheet($burl.'modules/mod_c7dialogmod
                    /jquery/theme/theme_darkness/ui.all.css');
          break;
  case trontastic:
        $document->addStyleSheet($burl.'modules/mod_c7dialogmod
                    /jquery/theme/theme_trontastic/ui.all.css');
          break;
  case southstreet:
        $document->addStyleSheet($burl.'modules/mod_c7dialogmod
                    /jquery/theme/theme_southstreet/ui.all.css');
          break;
  case swankypurse:
        $document->addStyleSheet($burl.'modules/mod_c7dialogmod
                    /jquery/theme/theme_swankypurse/ui.all.css');
          break;
```

```
default:
        $document->addStyleSheet($burl.'modules/mod_c7dialogmod
                        /jquery/theme/ui.all.css');
        break;
}
```

What the module is doing here is quite easy to see. The switch structure is using the $c7dialogmod_theme variable to decide which theme to load. As we want to use the theme selected in our SC jQuery plugin, the following changes need to be made:

```
$app =& JFactory::getApplication();

if( !$app->get('jquery') ){

  switch ($c7dialogmod_theme)
    {
  case lightness:
  .
  .
  . The rest of the code would be here
  .
  .
  default:
        $document->addStyleSheet($burl.'modules/mod_c7dialogmod
                        /jquery/theme/ui.all.css');
        break;
    }
}
```

Mostly, the only thing we need to do is envelop the previous code between our already well-known code:

```
$app =& JFactory::getApplication();

if( !$app->get('jquery') ){
  //The rest of the code would be here
}
```

This will solve the theme part; now, to the libraries load part. Reading down the code we will see the following code:

```
$document->addScript($burl.'modules/mod_c7dialogmod
            /jquery/jquery-1.3.2.js');

$document->addCustomTag('<script type="text/javascript">
            jQuery.noConflict();</script>');
```

```
$document->addScript($burl.'modules/mod_c7dialogmod
            /jquery/ui.core.js');

$document->addScript($burl.'modules/mod_c7dialogmod
            /jquery/ui.dialog.js');

$document->addScript($burl.'modules/mod_c7dialogmod
            /jquery/ui.draggable.js');

$document->addScript($burl.'modules/mod_c7dialogmod
            /jquery/ui.resizable.js');
```

Here we can see how the jQuery library is invoked, and then the `noConflict` method, and after all the jQuery UI part, the always essential core. Later the dialog, draggable, and resizable scripts are loaded. These are all necessary to show the dialog, drag it, and resize it.

All these library loads are not needed, as all of them are included in the SC jQuery library load. Just envelop it as follows:

```
if( !$app->get('jquery') ){
  $document->addScript($burl.'modules/mod_c7dialogmod
            /jquery/jquery-1.3.2.js');

  $document->addCustomTag('<script type="text/javascript">
            jQuery.noConflict();</script>');

  $document->addScript($burl.'modules/mod_c7dialogmod
            /jquery/ui.core.js');

  $document->addScript($burl.'modules/mod_c7dialogmod
            /jquery/ui.dialog.js');

  $document->addScript($burl.'modules/mod_c7dialogmod
            /jquery/ui.draggable.js');

  $document->addScript($burl.'modules/mod_c7dialogmod
            /jquery/ui.resizable.js');

}
```

Done! To the next one!

jQuery tabs module

This is our last extension; no more modifications will be needed. You have been doing a great job, so keep up with it. But first take a look at the extension we are talking about in the following screenshot:

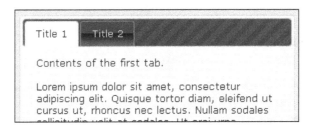

This extension will also be extremely easy to modify, just open the `modules/mod_jtabs/mod_jtabs.php` and read down the code until you find:

```
<script type="text/javascript"
        src="<?php echo JURI::root(); ?>
        modules/mod_jtabs/jquery/jquery.no.conflict.js">
</script>

<script type="text/javascript"
        src="<?php echo JURI::root(); ?>
        modules/mod_jtabs/jquery/jquery.min.js">
</script>

<script type="text/javascript"
        src="<?php echo JURI::root(); ?>
        modules/mod_jtabs/jquery/jquery-ui.min.js">
</script>

<link rel="stylesheet"
      href="<?php echo JURI::root(); ?>
      modules/mod_jtabs/jquery/jquery-ui.css" type="text/css" />
```

This module loads the libraries and the theme in the body part of our site, exactly in the module position where the module is loaded. It's important to note that, as the module is called after other modules, its style files, and the theme, will prevail over the previously loaded modules. We are going to solve this.

This time, for a change, we only need to envelop this code as follows:

```
<?php
  $app =& JFactory::getApplication();
  if( !$app->get('jquery') ){
?>

<script type="text/javascript" src="<?php echo JURI::root();
  ?>modules/mod_jtabs/jquery/jquery.no.conflict.js"></script>
<script type="text/javascript" src="<?php echo JURI::root();
  ?>modules/mod_jtabs/jquery/jquery.min.js"></script>
<script type="text/javascript" src="<?php echo JURI::root();
  ?>modules/mod_jtabs/jquery/jquery-ui.min.js"></script>
<link rel="stylesheet" href="<?php echo JURI::root(); ?>modules/
  mod_jtabs/jquery/jquery-ui.css" type="text/css" />

<?php
  }
?>
```

But hey, don't run away in happiness! There's still some modification necessary. A bit down in the code file, we can see:

```
$(function() {
  $("#tabs").tabs
```

We need to change that to:

```
jQuery(document).ready(function($) {
```

Why's that done? It's because the SC jQuery plugin sets jQuery to the no conflict mode. So the $ may not be available, and thus we need to use `jQuery` instead.

Phew! That has been quite a lot of work. But we are done, and we have reduced a lot of jQuery library loads. In fact if all has gone OK, and we will have the library loaded only once.

But continue reading, there's still more work to do.

Removing MooTools

At this point you may think that this is not necessary, as the SC jQuery plugin loaded the jQuery library with the "no conflict" mode, and we had no problems between the libraries.

But at the moment we aren't using the MooTools library. So, why load it? Anyway, we are going to see a way of removing the MooTools library. There are lots of other ways out there. Later, you will be able to decide if you want to remove it or not.

So let's get started; we will do this in our template. Open the `templates/jj15/index.php` file. In the template we have the following code:

```
<jdoc:include type="head" />
<?php JHTML::_('behavior.mootools'); ?>
```

Replace this code with:

```
<?php
  $headerstuff = $this->getHeadData();

  unset($headerstuff['scripts']['/media/system/js/mootools.js']);

  unset($headerstuff['scripts']['/media/system/js/caption.js']);

  $this->setHeadData($headerstuff);
?>

<jdoc:include type="head" />
```

What are we doing here? First we get all the header data:

```
$headerstuff = $this->getHeadData();
```

If we do this:

```
print_r($headerstuff)
```

In the code, we will see something similar to the following:

```
[scripts] => Array (
    [/plugins/system/scjquery/js/jquery-1.3.2.min.js] =>
      text/javascript
    [/plugins/system/scjquery/js/jquery.no.conflict.js] =>
      text/javascript
    [/plugins/system/scjquery/js/jquery-ui-1.7.2.custom.min.js] =>
      text/javascript
    [/media/system/js/mootools.js] => text/javascript
    [/media/system/js/caption.js] => text/javascript
    [/plugins/content/ppgallery/res/jquery.prettyPhoto.js"
      charset="utf-8] => text/javascript )
```

These scripts were added to the header data in the extensions we have seen, using the following:

```
$document->addscript
```

By reading the header data, we are able to remove the scripts that we don't want without modifying the Joomla! Core:

```
unset($headerstuff['scripts']['/media/system/js/mootools.js']);

unset($headerstuff['scripts']['/media/system/js/caption.js']);
```

After we have done all of the necessary modifications we can set the header data and call it with the `jdoc:include type="head"` tag, as follows:

```
$this->setHeadData($headerstuff);
?>

<jdoc:include type="head" />
```

And that's all. Now our site will load even faster. However, when we need MooTools we can easily turn it on again—quick and easy!

Tips and tricks

At this point, we must all agree that the SC jQuery plugin has been of great help to us. With very little effort we have been able to detect if the jQuery library has been loaded, and with that knowledge, decide whether to load it or not.

However, at this point, the SC jQuery plugin provides us with the following jQuery and jQuery UI versions:

- `jquery-1.3.2.min.js`
- `jquery-ui-1.7.2`

What can we do if we want to use newer versions? Some possibilities are as follows:

- Wait until a newer version of the SC jQuery plugin is available
- Directly link the jQuery library in our template with a `<script>` tag, without using the SC jQuery plugin

This last option is also quite easy to accomplish, and is the one we are going to follow in this tip. First, we need to open the `plugins/system/scjquery.php` file. Inside this file we are going to search for jQuery:

```
if ( file_exists( $file_path . 'js' . DS . 'jquery-1.3.2.min.js' ) &&
    file_exists( $file_path . 'js' . DS . 'jquery.no.conflict.js' ) ) {

    $doc =& JFactory::getDocument();

    $doc->addScript( $url_path . 'js/jquery-1.3.2.min.js' );
    $doc->addScript( $url_path . 'js/jquery.no.conflict.js' );
```

Here we can see how the plugin is first checking for the files, and then if they exist, using the `$doc->addScript` to load them in the header section of our site. If we want to use another library version, we first need to modify these lines.

Assume that we are going to use jQuery version 1.4.1, that uses a file such as `jquery-1.4.1.min.js`. In this case, we should change the previous code as follows:

```
if ( file_exists( $file_path . 'js' . DS . 'jquery-1.4.1.min.js' ) &&
file_exists( $file_path . 'js' . DS . 'jquery.no.conflict.js' ) ) {

    $doc =& JFactory::getDocument();

    $doc->addScript( $url_path . 'js/jquery-1.4.1.min.js' );
    $doc->addScript( $url_path . 'js/jquery.no.conflict.js' );
```

We also need to place the `jquery-1.4.1.min.js` file inside the `plugins/system/scjquery/js` folder. After that we should check our site, just to see that everything is still working.

 This is important as some extensions can stop working due to version changes. However, turning back the modifications we have made is something that can be done with very little work.

Luckily for us our site is working perfectly, and if we check the source code we will see:

```
<script type="text/javascript"
        src="/plugins/system/scjquery/js/jquery-1.4.1.min.js">
</script>
<script type="text/javascript"
        src="/plugins/system/scjquery/js/jquery.no.conflict.js">
</script>
```

We are using the new jQuery version. The process for changing the jQuery UI version is mostly the same. Say we want to use the `jquery-ui-1.8rc1` version, we will look for the following code:

```
if ( file_exists( $file_path . 'js' . DS .
                 'jquery-ui-1.7.2.custom.min.js' )
  && file_exists( $file_path . 'css' .DS . 'ui-lightness' . DS .
               'jquery-ui-1.7.2.custom.css' ) ) {

  $doc->addStylesheet( $url_path . 'css/' . $ui_theme .
                    '/jquery-ui-1.7.2.custom.css' );

  $doc->addScript( $url_path . 'js/jquery-ui-1.7.2.custom.min.js' );
```

And, if the file we are going to use is called `jquery-ui.min.js`, we change the previous code to look as follows:

```
if ( file_exists( $file_path . 'js' . DS . 'jquery-ui.min.js' )
  && file_exists( $file_path . 'css' .DS . 'ui-lightness' . DS .
               'jquery-ui-1.7.2.custom.css' ) ) {

  $doc->addStylesheet( $url_path . 'css/' . $ui_theme .
                    '/jquery-ui-1.7.2.custom.css' );

  $doc->addScript( $url_path . 'js/jquery-ui.min.js' );
```

Of course, we need to place the `jquery-ui.min.js` file inside the `plugins/system/scjquery/js` folder.

We are done updating our libraries, which is also very easy to do. But what if we want to add a new theme to use? If we look in the `plugins/system/scjquery/css` folder, we will see all the available themes. Say, for example, we want to add a theme called "excite-bike", which is not present in the plugin by default.

In this case, we will copy the `excite-bike` folder into our `plugins/system/scjquery/css` folder.

Of all the files inside the `excite-bike` folder, we only need the `jquery-ui.css` file, as it contains all the styles necessary.

We can delete all the other files, except the `images` folder. We also need to rename the `jquery-ui.css` file to `jquery-ui-1.7.2.custom.css`, as the plugin tries to open the themes by that name:

```
  $doc->addStylesheet( $url_path . 'css/' . $ui_theme .
                    '/jquery-ui-1.7.2.custom.css' );
```

It's easier to change one file's name than to change all the other ones.

Now, once we are done with those changes, if we go to our administrator screen and then to **Extensions | Plugin Manager | System - SC jQuery**, we will be able to select the new theme, as follows:

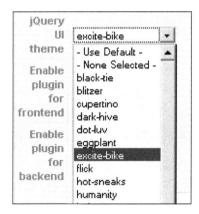

In this way we can add as many themes as we want. Why don't you try to add some now?

Summary

I think this has been a quite an interesting chapter and we have done a great job. As a result, our site now loads faster, we have removed the unnecessary library loads, and we have centralized the jQuery UI library styles.

This not only lets our site load faster, but also saves bandwidth and, more importantly, reduces the possibility of errors.

With all these changes, we have laid the necessary foundations to improve our site in the next chapters. Now we can go on without any problems. Ready? Let's go.

6
Getting Our Hands on Coding JavaScript

"Our first step on the ladder"

Yes! As promised in the previous chapters, this time we are going to get some coding done. This will be an interesting change as we will be able to see the results of our own coding. Of course, we are still going to use some libraries. But hey, we don't want to reinvent the wheel just because some of the effects we want to achieve are quite complex.

For now we are going to make all these modifications directly to the template. I think this is the easiest way to start. Later on we will make our own modules and components.

The points we are going to cover in this chapter are:

- Adding a Parallax effect to our template
- jQuery library jScrollPane
- Adding useful tooltips

As always, we seek to make our site more interesting through all these effects and utilities. But this time there's something more — we are also seeking to have a good time modifying our template. Coding can be fun! Don't believe me? Let's start and you'll see in a moment.

Adding movement to our site's header—Parallax effect

For this first modification, we are going to work with one of my favorite effects, the Parallax effect. We are going to use this in our header. If you remember our template, our header look like this:

Though this header looks fine with our template (I did it myself, so don't be a critic), we want something more eye-catching. We are going to change this header to a Parallax-powered one.

If you have never seen a Parallax effect, I think we can describe it as a mimic of a 3D effect. It basically consists of some images, each one on top of the other. We can use this to create an illusion of distance. We can see this better with a representation, as shown in the following picture:

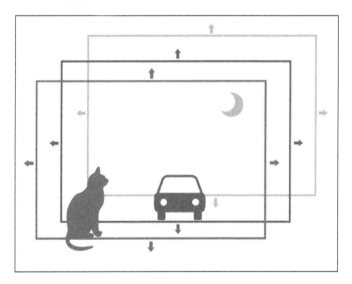

As we can see there are three elements in the image: a cat, a car, and the moon. The cat is in the first instance, then the car, and at the bottom is the moon. Each one of these elements looks smaller than the previous one, though we know that the moon is bigger than a cat.

This is what forms the perspective, letting us know that the cat is nearer than the moon and thus creating the 3D effect that we are seeking.

Preparing the HTML necessary for our example

In order to achieve this effect, we will need to complete some steps. But first, take a look at our site's code so that we can later appreciate the differences. Just open the `templates/jj15/index.php` file and search for the next piece of code inside this file:

```
<div id="header">
  <div id="login">
    <jdoc:include type="modules" name="login" />
  </div>
  <img src="<?php echo $this->baseurl?>/templates/jj15/images/
    header_image.gif" />
</div><!-- End of header -->
```

As we can see, in this little piece of code, we were declaring a DIV and placing a simple image inside it. Forget about the `login` DIV, it doesn't really matter for this example.

This was quite simple as we really don't need to do anything else. The CSS for this header DIV is also quite simple. Take a look at the `templates/jj15/css/styles.css` file:

```
#header{
  height: 58px;
  position: relative;
}
```

We only need to add the `height` of the DIV and the relative positioning. All this code is quite simple and, though we are not going to complicate things too much, we do need to make some changes.

But first, let me present the images that we are going to use. The following image is the background:

The next image is the middle section; it will feature some small ninjas:

And the following image with some mountains and trees is for the front part:

Nice, aren't they? Why don't you take a look at them in the code bundle? They are placed in the Chapter 6 folder and are named `parallax_1.png`, `parallax_2.png`, and `parallax_3.png`.

These images were made for me by Fairhead Creative, and we are going to put these images to use right now. Place them inside the `templates/jj15/images` folder.

Now, if you haven't opened it yet, open the `templates/jj15/index.php` file and replace the following code:

```
<div id="header">
  <div id="login">
    <jdoc:include type="modules" name="login" />
  </div>
  <img src="<?php echo $this->baseurl?>/templates/jj15/images/
     header_image.gif" />
</div><!-- End of header -->
```

Replace it with the following code:

```
<div id="header">
  <div id="login">
    <jdoc:include type="modules" name="login" />
  </div>
  <ul id="parallax">
      <li id="parallax_bottom"> </li>
      <li id="parallax_middle"> </li>
      <li id="parallax_top"> </li>
  </ul>
</div>
```

 This code, the CSS that will come next, and even the JavaScript, can be found inside the code bundle, so take a look in the folder for Chapter 6.

It's not much different from the previous one, is it? We have created an `ul` list with some `li` elements inside. Each one of these `li` elements will contain one of the images we have seen before. How are we going to place them? With a little bit of CSS help.

Open the `templates/jj15/css/styles.css` file; we are going to add some CSS rules at the bottom:

```css
/**
 * Parallax effect
 */

#parallax{
    position: relative;
}

#parallax_bottom{
    position: absolute;
    z-index: 3001;
    width: 980px;
    height: 57px;
    background-image: url('../images/parallax_3.png');
    background-repeat: no-repeat;
}

#parallax_middle{
    position: absolute;
    z-index: 3002;
    width: 980px;
    height: 57px;
    background-image: url('../images/parallax_2.png');
    background-repeat: no-repeat;
}

#parallax_top{
     position: absolute;
    z-index: 3003;
    width: 980px;
    height: 57px;
    background-image: url('../images/parallax_1.png');
    background-repeat: no-repeat;
}
```

Here we are not only giving the elements a z-index value, width, and height, but are also, very importantly, placing each image inside each element. Now, if all has gone okay, on our site we will see something similar to the following screenshot:

As you can see, we have accomplished our task of putting the image one on top of the other, but the problem is that the login button has been covered. There is nothing that some CSS can't solve, just search for this code in the CSS file:

```css
#login{
  position: absolute;
  right: 0;
  z-index: 1;
}
```

Give a z-index greater than the other elements, for example, 3004, as follows:

```css
#login{
  position: absolute;
  right: 0;
  z-index: 3004;
}
```

Now the login button will return to its previous location, in front of all the other elements, so our visitors can click on it:

Adding jQuery Parallax library

Now you might be thinking, "hey, it's nice, but not much different from how it was before," and you'd be right. However, at this point we are going to introduce the JavaScript part.

The first thing we need to do is download the Parallax plugin. This time we are going to use the "jQuery Parallax" plugin. We can find it at the following URL:

http://plugins.jquery.com/project/jquery-parallax-style.

Or, you can search for "parallax" in the plugins section of the jQuery site. Once you get there, download the plugin.

Inside the plugin file you will find a file called `jquery.parallax-0.2-min.js`. Place it inside the `templates/jj15/js` folder.

Now we need to link the script in the header of our template—the `templates/jj15/index.php` file:

```
<jdoc:include type="head" />

<script type="text/javascript" src="<?php echo $this->baseurl ?>
/templates/jj15//js/jquery.parallax-0.2-min.js"></script>
```

This will load the plugin, and let us use it to create the effect. We are not loading the jQuery library. Remember that as we are using the SC jQuery Joomla! plugin, we don't need to load the jQuery library.

If we weren't using this Joomla! plugin, or another similar one, we would need to load the jQuery library in a similar manner.

After linking the script, we are going to also link one script of our own. We will call it `parallax.js` and link it as follows:

```
<jdoc:include type="head" />

<script type="text/javascript" src="<?php echo $this->baseurl ?>
    /templates/jj15//js/jquery.parallax-0.2-min.js"></script>

<script type="text/javascript" src="<?php echo $this->baseurl ?>
    /templates/jj15//js/parallax.js"></script>
```

However, we need to create this file, and also create it inside the `templates/jj15/js` folder. Call it `parallax.js` and inside it place the following code:

```
jQuery(document).ready(function($) {
    $('#parallax').parallax({
        'elements': [
          {
            'selector': '#parallax_bottom',
            'properties': {
              'x': {
                'background-position-x': {
                  'initial': 0,
                  'multiplier': 0
                }
              }
```

```
                }
            },
            {
                'selector': '#parallax_middle',
                'properties': {
                    'x': {
                        'background-position-x': {
                            'initial': 0,
                            'multiplier': 0.1,
                            'invert': true
                        }
                    }
                }
            },
            {
                'selector': '#parallax_top',
                'properties': {
                    'x': {
                        'background-position-x': {
                            'initial': 0,
                            'multiplier': 0.2
                        }
                    }
                }
            }
        ]
    });
});
```

Now that's quite a bit of code, but most of it is quite easy to understand. Let's take a look at some pieces of it:

```
$('#parallax').parallax
```

This code adds the Parallax effect to the element with the `parallax` ID. Then we have the elements array:

```
'elements':
```

Here we can define the properties and values of each element. Each one of the mentioned elements is created more or less as follows:

```
{
    'selector': '#parallax_bottom',
    'properties': {
        'x': {
```

```
        'background-position-x': {
            'initial': 0,
            'multiplier': 0
        }
    }
  }
}
```

First goes the selector, where we indicate the element we are talking about, and then the property. In our case, we are working with the x property. This is because our elements are only going to be moved horizontally.

Later, we define values for the background position; those values are:

- `initial` — is the starting position for the background element. For our background, we are going to select 0.

- `multiplier` — defines the quantity of movement. The greater the number the more our elements will be moved.

- `invert` — with this we can select if the elements will move in the mouse direction (`false`) or not (`true`).

 There are some other options, but for our example these three will work okay. If you want to go deeper into this plugin, you can take a look at:

http://www.dom111.co.uk/blog/coding/jquery-parallax-0-2-minor-updates/125.

But first, take a look at the result — check the next image:

I've tried to capture the image in another position, but the best way of checking it is by trying it yourself. So why don't you give it a try? Remember you can find the code and images in the code bundle, so you can try this effect in no time. You will only need to download the plugin from the creator's page.

Tips and tricks

You may have noticed that we have used transparent PNG images to achieve this effect. Most modern browsers will have no problems with transparencies, but some old ones, like IE 6 may be unable to show these transparencies.

However, we can use a plugin like **IFixPng improved** to solve these problems. You can find this plugin at:

`http://plugins.jquery.com/project/iFixPng2.`

Like the other module, it can be searched for on the jQuery site, and with its help, we can solve the transparency problems under IE 6.

Now we are done with the Parallax effect. Did you like it? Then get ready for the next one.

jQuery library jScrollPane

This is another extension that I like a lot. I know I'm always telling you that the extensions and plugins we see are great. But I hope you agree with me.

The developers of these extensions have done great work with them, and I think I'm very enthusiastic in developing our site. But enough talk, let's continue with our work.

This time we are going to see the jScrollPane plugin. With this plugin, we will be able to create a scrollbar in any DIV we want.

For example, take a look at the central module zones on our site:

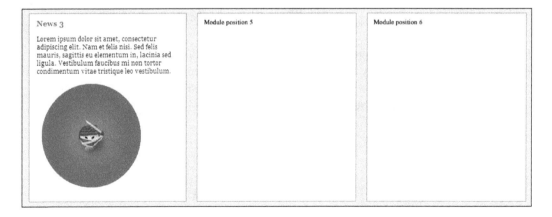

Those zones are quite practical, though a bit small. If we place a large amount of text on them, we may not be able to see all of it. Let's try it! Just open the Administrator screen of our site; then we can go to **Extensions | Module Manager**, and then click on **New** and later on **Custom HTML**.

Place this module in the **module_5** position of our template. Then add some demo content to it. It should look more or less as follows:

Lorem ipsum dolor sit amet, consectetur adipiscing elit. Integer euismod luctus nisi eget ullamcorper. In in tellus ligula, at malesuada sem. Suspendisse magna dolor, dictum a posuere eu, vehicula ut ligula. Nunc ultricies blandit molestie. Etiam malesuada, est commodo blandit tempor, dolor metus laoreet velit, id adipiscing felis elit non mauris. Morbi suscipit nisi at ligula consequat tincidunt. Curabitur commodo, odio non fringilla malesuada, nunc neque faucibus diam, eget consequat velit orci a mauris. Donec malesuada tortor vel ante tristique fringilla. Vestibulum erat orci, tempor non varius at, euismod at lorem. Aenean feugiat quam a leo dictum egestas. Duis sed ullamcorper eros. Aliquam nisi sem, tempus eget ornare eget, tristique eu nisi. Cum sociis natoque penatibus et magnis dis parturient montes, nascetur ridiculus mus. Quisque eu volutpat orci. Suspendisse libero lacus, sollicitudin non tincidunt quis, faucibus a eros.

Vestibulum semper varius augue nec vehicula.

Here you can see an example of exactly what we were talking about. When we have quite a long paragraph of text, we need more space for it to be shown. But we don't have the space. Wouldn't it be great to incorporate a scroll bar, not the browser ones, but better ones that looked like the rest of our site, with the same style and look?

Get ready! That's just what we are going to do. First, we need to download the plugin. We can look for it in the jQuery page by performing a search for "jScrollPane", or by visiting the developer's site:

http://www.kelvinluck.com/assets/jquery/jScrollPane/jScrollPane.html.

Once downloaded, the steps to have our scroll bar ready are a few. But let's go step by step. First search for the jScrollPane.js file, or something similar—the version number really doesn't matter.

This file needs to be placed in the templates/jj15/js folder, and as in the previous examples, we need to add a script tag in our template header:

```
<script type="text/javascript" src="<?php echo $this->baseurl ?>
/templates/jj15/js/jScrollPane.js"></script>
```

With this done, we also need to link another file—this time a CSS file. Look for a file called `jScrollPane.css` or similar. This file contains the basic styles for the plugin to work. So we need to place it in our `templates/jj15/css` folder.

Later in our template, we need to include it as follows:

```
<link rel="stylesheet" href="<?php echo $this->baseurl ?>
    /templates/jj15/css/jScrollPane.css" type="text/css" />
```

We now have the basic files ready, but we need to make some changes to our template file. Open the `templates/jj15/index.php` file. If you are going to use the `module_5` position, search for the following code:

```
<?php if($this->countModules('module_5')) : ?>
<div id="module_5">
  <div class="pad">
    <jdoc:include type="modules" name="module_5" />
  </div>
</div><!-- End module 5 -->
<?php endif; ?>
```

We can modify this code as follows:

```
<?php if($this->countModules('module_5')) : ?>
<div id="module_5">
    <div class="pad">
        <div id="scroll_1">
          <jdoc:include type="modules" name="module_5" />
        </div>
    </div>
</div><!-- End module 5 -->
<?php endif; ?>
```

We are almost done. We only need to make the function call. The basic way is as follows:

```
<?php if($this->countModules('module_5')) : ?>
<div id="module_5">
    <div class="pad">
        <div id="scroll_1">
          <jdoc:include type="modules" name="module_5" />
        </div>
    </div>
</div><!-- End module 5 -->
    <script type="text/javascript">
      jQuery(document).ready(function($) {
            $('#scroll_1').jScrollPane();
            });
    </script>
<?php endif; ?>
```

We call the `jScrollPane` function over our newly created `scroll_1` DIV. With this our site will look similar to the following screenshot:

Now our `scroll_1` DIV has a scrollbar applied to it, but somehow disappears at the bottom. This is because of the DIV height. Well, as we haven't defined a height for our DIV, it uses the limits of the `module_5` DIV. Let's give it a height in our template's `css/styles.css` file:

```
#scroll_1{
    height: 322px;
}
```

With this little modification, our module position will look similar to the following image:

Lorem ipsum dolor sit amet, consectetur adipiscing elit. Integer euismod luctus nisi eget ullamcorper. In in tellus ligula, at malesuada sem. Suspendisse magna dolor, dictum a posuere eu, vehicula ut ligula. Nunc ultricies blandit molestie. Etiam malesuada, est commodo blandit tempor, dolor metus laoreet velit, id adipiscing felis elit non mauris. Morbi suscipit nisi at ligula consequat tincidunt. Curabitur commodo, odio non fringilla malesuada, nunc neque faucibus diam, eget consequat velit orci a mauris. Donec malesuada tortor vel ante tristique fringilla. Vestibulum erat orci, tempor non varius at, euismod at lorem. Aenean feugiat quam a leo dictum egestas. Duis sed ullamcorper eros. Aliquam nisi sem, tempus eget ornare eget, tristique eu nisi. Cum sociis natoque penatibus et magnis dis parturient montes, nascetur ridiculus mus. Quisque eu volutpat orci. Suspendisse libero lacus,

Now we can notice the difference between the slider track and the drag. It is much better now, isn't it?

But we can also modify the style a bit, and this is quite easy to achieve. For example, add the following styles to the template's css/styles.css file:

```
.jScrollPaneDrag {
  background: #B40000;
}

.jScrollPaneTrack {
  background: #DADADA;
}
```

Now our module will look like the next screenshot:

It is important to note that these styles modify the base styles. Therefore, we need to load our stylesheet after the jScrollPane, as follows:

```
<link rel="stylesheet" href="<?php echo $this->baseurl
?>/templates/jj15/css/jScrollPane.css" type="text/css" />
<link rel="stylesheet" href="<?php echo $this->baseurl
?>/templates/jj15/css/styles.css" type="text/css" />
```

Do you think we are done? No, we can still do more.

Adding mouse scrolling

Wouldn't it be nice to have scrolling capabilities in our scroll? Sure it would, and as it's something easy to achieve, we are going to do it. If you have downloaded the jScrollPane bundle, inside you will find a file called `jquery.mousewheel.js`. If not, you can download this useful plugin from:

`http://plugins.jquery.com/project/mousewheel`.

Or, search the jQuery site for "mouse wheel extension". Once we have a copy of the plugin, we need to place it in the template's `js` folder and then link it in our header, as in our previous examples:

```
<script type="text/javascript" src="<?php echo $this->baseurl ?>
/templates/jj15/js/jquery.mousewheel.js"></script>
```

After we have done so, we will be able to scroll with our mouse wheel.

We are done with the jScrollPane plugin, and I encourage you to check all the possible options on their site:

`http://www.kelvinluck.com/assets/jquery/jScrollPane/jScrollPane.html`.

There are lots of great possibilities. Just check them!

Adding useful tooltips

This is going to be our last example for this chapter. But don't worry, I know we have already worked a lot, so this last example is going to be quite easy and short.

Tooltips are always a good way of adding hints and info. Interested visitors can see this info, but visitors who are not interested don't need to see this info.

A tooltip plugin that looks pretty good is the **Coda Bubble** plugin. As with the other plugins, we can search for it on the jQuery site, or at the following link:

`http://plugins.jquery.com/project/codabubble`.

If we want to download it, we can do so from the developers' site:

`http://www.myjquery.co.uk/`.

After downloading the coda bubble ZIP file, we have all the files needed. So let's get started. A place where a tooltip can be of help is the footer. At this point in time, our site footer looks as follows:

Not much info, well, in fact no info. We can take more advantage of our footer, giving some more information to our visitors or placing any message we want. For example, look in our `templates/jj15/index.php` file; at the very bottom of it, we can read:

```
</div><!-- End footer wrapper -->
```

Just before this, we are going to add some text:

```
<br/><br/>
    <p class="info">Demo site created for the Joomla!
        javascript jQuery Packt book +info</p>
</div><!-- End footer wrapper -->
```

We need some styles before we can take a look into this. In the `templates/jj15/styles.css` file, at the end we will add:

```
/**
* Coda Bubble
*/

.info{
    color: #ffffff;
    text-align: center;
}
```

There's not much styling, but it will make our text look a bit better, as we can see in our next screenshot:

Now we are going to follow the steps necessary to create a tooltip on the **+info** word. Stay with me, it's going to be interesting! First, as always, we need to include the plugin JavaScript file so that we can use it later.

After downloading and uncompressing the plugin bundle, we will find a file called `jquery.codabubble.js`, or something similar. Where do you think we are going to place this file? Exactly! In `templates/jj15/js/jquery.codabubble.js`. Also, don't forget to create the `script` tag in the header of our template.

But we will also need a CSS file with all the styles necessary for the tooltip to work. The file we are talking about is `bubble.css` — we can't get lost on this. Take it and place it in `templates/jj15/css`.

This CSS file also needs some images to work. These images are located in a folder called `images` and we are going to place this folder inside `templates/jj15/css` too.

It would be nice to rename this folder as something more useful for us to remember what is inside it. For example, we can have something similar to `templates/jj15/css/bubble_images`.

 Remember that if we rename the folder, we will need to open the `bubble.css` file and change all appearances of the images folder to `bubble_images`.

Don't forget to add the `include` tag in our header:

```
<link rel="stylesheet" href="<?php echo $this->baseurl ?>/templates/
    jj15/css/bubble.css" type="text/css" />
```

The styles now get included. After that, we will add some text, which will go into the tooltip. We can place it in any way we want, even include images. For now we are going to place something simple, as follows:

```
<br/><br/>
<p class="info">Demo site created for the Joomla! javascript jQuery
Packt book +info</p>
<div class="bubble_html">
    Author: Jose Argudo Blanco.<br/>
    Title: Joomla! Javascript jQuery.<br/>
    Theme: Joomla!, jQuery.<br/>
    Publisher: Packt Publishing.<br/>
    Contact: jose@joseargudo.com
</div>
```

The important thing here is to have the `bubble_html` class in our DIV. Inside this DIV, the `jquery.codabubble.js` will search for the content to show inside the tooltip. Are there other changes that need to be done? It seems so. Well, at the end, our code must look as follows:

```
<br/><br/>
<div class="coda_bubble">
    <p class="info">Demo site created for the Joomla! javascript
        jQuery Packt book <span class="trigger">+info</span></p>
    <div class="bubble_html">
            Author: Jose Argudo Blanco.<br/>
            Title: Joomla! Javascript jQuery.<br/>
            Theme: Joomla!, jQuery.<br/>
            Publisher: Packt Publishing.<br/>
            Contact: jose@joseargudo.com
    </div>
</div>
```

Let's take a look at these elements. We can see that all the code is enveloped in a DIV with the `coda_bubble` class. Inside this DIV, we can find the two tooltip elements:

- `trigger` — the trigger class will contain the element that will make the call to action when the mouse pointer is over it
- `bubble_html` — contains the text, images, and much more, which is going to appear inside the tooltip

We can have as many `coda_bubble` DIVs as we want — each one with his own pair of `trigger` and `bubble_html`. Now that the structure is ready, what we need to do is execute the call, with something like the following:

```
            Contact: jose@joseargudo.com
        </div>
</div>
<script type="text/javascript">
        jQuery(document).ready(function($) {
        opts = {
                distances : [20],
                leftShifts : [280],
                bubbleTimes : [500],
                hideDelays : [0],
                bubbleWidths : [300],
                bubbleImagesPath : "<?php echo $this->baseurl
                ?>/templates/jj15/css/bubble_images/skins/classic",
                msieFix : true,
                msiePop : true
```

```
        };
    $('.coda_bubble').codaBubble(opts);
    });
</script>
```

Let's take a look at these parameters:

- `distances` — defines the distance from the tooltip to the trigger, in height
- `leftshifts` — indicates the distance of the tooltip to the left of the DIV
- `bubbletimes` — as its name suggests, it indicates how long the tooltip will be active
- `hidedelays` — defines how long the tooltip will last once the mouse pointer is out of the trigger
- `bubblewidths` — lets us establish the width of the tooltip
- `BubbleImagesPath` — indicates the route to the images that are going to be used in the tooltip
- `msieFix` — when Internet Explorer is detected, instead of using PNGs of the images directory, it uses GIF images
- `msiepop` — if set to `false`, tooltips will not be shown on Internet Explorer

And those were the parameters. Pretty easy, aren't they? You can get all the details and examples of these parameters at the following link:

`http://www.myjquery.co.uk/docs/x/plugins/coda_bubble/coda_bubble.php`.

Before finishing, and to make the styles look better, I've made a small change to the `templates/jj15/css/bubbles.css` file. We need to change the following style:

```
.coda_bubble {
    position: relative;
    top: 0px;
    left: 0px;
    width:100px;
    text-align:left;
    float:left;
    padding-left:20px;
}
```

It needs to be modified as follows:

```
.coda_bubble {
    position: relative;
    width: 414px;
    margin: 0 auto;
}
```

But this is just a style change that doesn't really affect the way the plugin works. It's time to take a look at the result of our work!

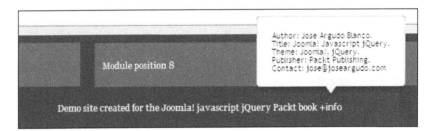

Quite nice, isn't it? Job done!

If you find problems with the library, it may be because we are using the SC jQuery Joomla! plugin with the no-conflict mode. The `jquery.codabubble.js` plugin doesn't works this way, but it's quite easy to solve that. Just open the `jquery.codabubble.js` file and change the `$` instances you find to `jQuery`. That's all! After that, the plugin will work like a charm.

Tips and tricks

Remember that we can change the images inside the `images` folder of the plugin in order to make them look better, along with our template. It only requires the time to create the necessary images.

Also, we can use any class we want instead of `coda_bubble`. Just remember to also rename the class found in the `bubble.css` file to match the name you use.

Don't forget to take a good look at the developer's site for more examples and other very useful tools!

Summary

This has been an engaging chapter, and I really hope you have enjoyed it. All the effects and plugins we have seen can be studied further. The possibilities of the Parallax effect are almost endless, and not much needs to be said about the scroller and tooltip plugins. These can be useful on almost any site.

However, in this chapter, I didn't want to show you everything about these plugins, but just show the things that can be achieved with jQuery, some other great plugins, and by working on just the template.

In the next chapter, we are going to create our own modules and extensions, but remember, a lot of work can also be done on the template. After the next chapters are over, it will be up to you to decide if you want to create an extension, modify the template, or search for an already developed extension.

We, as developers, designers, site-building fans, and so on, have an almost endless set of options. This is what I like about Joomla! and jQuery, and that's what I'm trying to show you in this book. Now take some rest, we will continue this conversation in the next chapter!

7
Creating Our Own Modules

"Packing together all of our efforts."

In the previous chapter, we saw how we could modify our template to enhance its appearance, or to add some useful features. Though that didn't take us too much time, if we want to apply these features to another site we will need to re-do all the work again.

Repeating the process again can be a waste of time and effort. Wouldn't it be better to create a module packing that feature? That way we can use the fruit of our work in a convenient way.

After all, if you remember the first few chapters of our book, it was pretty easy to download and install all those extensions that we now have on our site.

In this chapter, we are going to build a simple module, just a tiny contact form. We will build a basic foundation, and then enhance it with some nice features. Sadly, we can't make a full, thorough guide. We would need almost three entire chapters for that; so we will concentrate on the basic things.

But don't worry, there are lots of resources on building Joomla! Extensions. For example, there is the *Learning Joomla! 1.5 Extension Development* book from Packt. However, let's take a look at the content of the chapter. In this chapter, we will:

- Learn the basics of Joomla! module creation
- Create a "Send us a question" module
- Make a better form using JavaScript
    - Send the form using jQuery AJAX
    - Validate form fields using jQuery, and learn why it is important to validate
- Pack and install our module

Interested? Then don't wait, start right away!

Learning the basics of Joomla! module creation

Building a basic Joomla! module is not that difficult. In fact it's quite easy. Just stay with me, and we will divide the task into some easy-to-follow steps. First of all, we need to create a folder for our module, for example, `mod_littlecontact`. This folder is where we will place all the files necessary for our module.

For example, one of the files we are going to need is the `mod_littlecontact.php` file, which is named exactly the same as the folder, but with a `.php` extension. Let's see what we need to put in it:

```php
<?php
defined('_JEXEC') or die('Direct Access to this location is not
allowed.');
?>
<h1>Just a simple contact form!</h1>
```

We will look at just the basics. First, `defined('_JEXEC')` checks whether the file has been included by Joomla! instead of being called directly. If it has been included by Joomla!, the `_JEXEC` constant would have been defined.

With this PHP file created we need to create another file, an XML one this time. We will call it `mod_littlecontact.xml`; notice that, again, the name is the same as the folder one. Just create the file, and after that we will place the following contents in it:

```xml
<?xml version="1.0" encoding="utf-8"?>
<install type="module" version="1.5.0">

        <name>Little Contact Form</name>
        <author>Jose Argudo Blanco</author>
        <creationDate>2010</creationDate>
        <copyright>All rights reserved by Jose Argudo
                Blanco.</copyright>
        <license>GPL 2.0</license>
        <authorEmail>jose@joseargudo.com</authorEmail>
        <authorUrl>www.joseargudo.com</authorUrl>
        <version>1.0.0</version>
        <description>A simple contact form</description>
        <files>
            <filename module="mod_littlecontact">
                mod_littlecontact.php</filename>
        </files>
</install>
```

Most of the contents of this XML file are quite easy to follow and very self-explanatory. In the files section, we have included all the files necessary for our module. Notice that we do not include the XML file itself.

With these two files created, we can give a try to this simple module. Copying this folder into our Joomla! modules folder won't work, as Joomla! requires us to install the extension through the **Extensions | Install/Uninstall** menu. So, what do we need to do? Just compress these two files into a ZIP file by using any tool of your liking. At the end we will need to have a `mod_littlecontact.zip` file with the following two files inside:

- `mod_littlecontact.php`
- `mod_littlecontact.xml`

Installing our module is done exactly as with any other modules. Go to the administrator screen of our site, then go to the **Extensions | Install/Uninstall** menu, search and select the file, and then click on **Upload File & Install** button.

If all goes OK, and it really should, we will be able to find our module listed in **Extensions | Module Manager**, as seen in the following screenshot:

Little Contact Form

We can click in the module name, just as we would do with any of the others. If we enter the administration panel of the module we will see a screen very much like the other modules, as Joomla! standardizes this screen. Just take a look at the **Details** zone, which will look like the next screenshot:

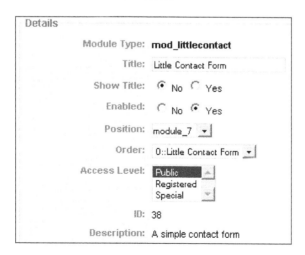

Here we can select the parameters we want, and enable the module. This time we will place it in the **module_7** position of our template. Also note that the description is the one that we place in the module XML file:

```
<description>A simple contact form</description>
```

After we have enabled the module, we will be able to see it in the frontend, in the module position we have selected:

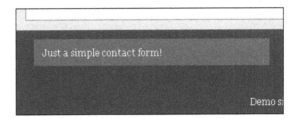

There's not too much for now, but it's working! Now we will enhance it and convert it into a contact form.

 Note that now that we have installed our module, a new folder will have been created into our Joomla! installation. We can find this folder in the `modules` folder, it will be called `mod_littlecontact`.

So now we have this structure on our Joomla! Site:

```
modules/
        mod_littlecontact/
                            mod_littlecontact.php
                            mod_littlecontact.xml
```

 As the module is already installed, we can modify these files, and we will be able to see the changes without needing to reinstall it.

We have just accomplished our first step; the basics are there, and now we can concentrate on making our modifications.

 You can find all this code in the code bundle, Chapter 7, in the folder called "Learning the basics". Take a look into it!

Creating a "Send us a question" module

One of the first things we are going to create is an empty `index.html` file; this will be used so that no one can take a look at the folder structure for the module. For example, imagine that our site is installed in `http://wayofthewebninja.com`. If we go to `http://wayofthewebninja.com/modules/mod_littlecontact/` we will see something like the next image:

Index of /modules/mod_littlecontact

- Parent Directory
- mod_littlecontact.php
- mod_littlecontact.xml

Apache Server at wayofthewebninja.com Port 80

If we try to click on `mod_littlecontact.php`, we will see the following phrase:

Direct Access to this location is not allowed.

That's because the code we added to our file is as follows:

```
<?php
defined('_JEXEC') or die('Direct Access to this location is not
allowed.');
?>
```

Of course, we don't want people to be able to see which files we are using for our module. For this place, we used the empty `index.html` file mentioned in the `modules/mod_littlecontact` folder.

This way, if anyone tries to go to `http://wayofthewebninja.com/modules/mod_littlecontact/`, they will see only an empty screen.

Good, now note that when we add any file, we need to reflect it on the `mod_littlecontact.xml` file in the `files` section:

```
<files>
  <filename
     module="mod_littlecontact">mod_littlecontact.php</filename>
    <filename>index.html</filename>
</files>
```

This way, when we pack the file for install, the installation process will take this file into account, otherwise it will be left out.

Once we have done this, we are going to create another file, a CSS one this time, so we can put our styles in it. For this we are going to first create a new folder, also called `css`. It will be placed in `modules/mod_littlecontact/`. Inside that folder we will create a file called `styles.css`; this file also needs to be declared in the XML:

```
<filename>css/styles.css</filename>
```

In this `modules/mod_littlecontact/css/styles.css` file we are going to place the following code:

```css
#littlecontact h1{
    font-size: 18px;
    border-bottom: 1px solid #ffffff;
}
```

But then, if we are to apply these styles, we need to load this CSS file. How are we going to do this? Open the `modules/mod_littlecontact/mod_littlecontact.php` file and modify it as follows:

```php
<?php
defined('_JEXEC') or die('Direct Access to this location is not
allowed.');

JHTML::stylesheet('styles.css','modules/mod_littlecontact/css/');

?>
<div id="littlecontact">
    <h1>Just a simple contact form!</h1>
</div>
```

There's not much change here; we have enveloped our previous content in a DIV, with the `littlecontact` ID, so that we can target our styles. This is the easy part, but there's also an important one, shown as follows:

```php
JHTML::stylesheet('styles.css','modules/mod_littlecontact/css/');
```

We are using the `JHTML::stylesheet` method to create a link, in our header section, to our CSS file. In fact, if we check the source code on our frontend, we will see:

```html
<link rel="stylesheet" href="/modules/mod_littlecontact/css/
styles.css" type="text/css" />
```

This way our stylesheet will be loaded, and our module will look like the next screenshot:

As we can see, our styles have been applied. The JHTML::stylesheet method is quite easy to use, the first parameter being the file and the second one being the path to the file.

Now we are going to prepare our simple form. Again we will modify our mod_littlecontact.php file, and now it will look more like the following:

```php
<?php
defined('_JEXEC') or die('Direct Access to this location is not
allowed.');

JHTML::stylesheet('styles.css','modules/mod_littlecontact/css/');

?>
<div id="littlecontact">
    <h1>Just a simple contact form!</h1>

    <form action="index.php" method="post" id="sc_form">

        <label>Your name:</label><br/>
        <input type="text" name="your_name" value="" size="40"
         class="sc_input"/><br/><br/>

        <label>Your question:</label><br/>
        <textarea name="your_question" class="sc_input" rows="5"
         cols="30"></textarea><br/><br/>

        <input type="submit" name="send" value="Send"
         class="sc_button" />

    </form>
</div>
```

This is a common HTML form. We need some styling here, just to make it look good. Let's make the following minimal changes to our `styles.css` file:

```css
#littlecontact h1{
    font-size: 18px;
    border-bottom: 1px solid #ffffff;
    margin-bottom: 15px;
}

.sc_input{
    border: 1px solid #3A362F;
}

.sc_button{
    background-color: #3A362F;
    border: 0;
    color: #ffffff;
    padding: 5px;
}
```

Most styles are new, and modifications to previous `h1` styling have been marked. With this minimal change our module looks a bit better.

You can see it in the following screenshot:

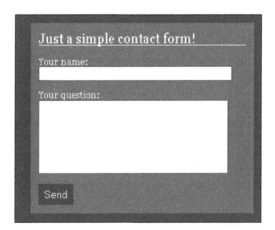

Good, now we are going to prepare the send part. Don't worry, this is not going to be hard. But first we will try to separate the logic from the presentation. This is just to have the PHP code and the HTML code separated — much like the way we separated the CSS and HTML.

In order to do this we are going to create another folder, this time called `tmpl`, the short form of `templates`. This way we will have `modules/mod_littlecontact/tmpl`.

Inside that folder we are going to create two files:

- `modules/mod_littlecontact/tmpl/default_tmpl.php`
- `modules/mod_littlecontact/tmpl/sendok_tmpl.php`

Let's start with the first one, `default_tmpl.php`:

```php
<?php
defined('_JEXEC') or die('Direct Access to this location is not
allowed.');
?>
<div id="littlecontact">
    <h1>Just a simple contact form!</h1>

    <form action="index.php" method="post" id="sc_form">

        <label>Your name:</label><br/>
        <input type="text" name="your_name" value="" size="40"
          class="sc_input"/><br/><br/>

        <label>Your question:</label><br/>
        <textarea name="your_question" class="sc_input" rows="5"
          cols="30"></textarea><br/><br/>

        <input type="submit" name="send" value="Send"
          class="sc_button" />

    </form>
</div>
```

We have just placed the form's HTML code in this file. What about the content of the `sendok_tmpl.php` file? Place the following code:

```php
<?php
defined('_JEXEC') or die('Direct Access to this location is not
allowed.');
?>
<div id="littlecontact">
    <h1>The form has been sent ok</h1>
</div>
```

This displays a message if everything is OK when the form is sent. Now don't forget to add the following files to our XML file:

```
<filename>tmpl/default_tmpl.php</filename>
<filename>tmpl/sendok_tmpl.php</filename>
```

Things are going well, and now we need to decide when to show which template. Just check the `mod_littlecontact.php` file and remove everything but the following code:

```php
<?php
defined('_JEXEC') or die('Direct Access to this location is not
allowed.');

JHTML::stylesheet('styles.css','modules/mod_littlecontact/css/');
?>
```

Now add the following code to the previous code:

```php
JHTML::stylesheet('styles.css','modules/mod_littlecontact/css/');

$form_send = JRequest::getVar('form_send', 'notsend');

switch($form_send){

    case 'send':
        require(JModuleHelper::getLayoutPath('mod_littlecontact',
                'sendok_tmpl'));
        break;

    default:
        require(JModuleHelper::getLayoutPath('mod_littlecontact',
                'default_tmpl'));

}

?>
```

There are some interesting things happening here; first we will try to retrieve a variable:

```php
$form_send = JRequest::getVar('form_send', 'notsend');
```

The `JRequest::getVar` method tries to get a variable from the `$_GET`, `$_POST`, `$_REQUEST`, `$_FILES`, or `$_COOKIE` arrays. The first parameter is the variable name we are expecting, and the second parameter is a default value. In the case that the variable is not set it will be initialized with the value we define here.

Once we have this variable we can use it as a `switch` to decide which template to load. But how is a template loaded? Very easily, as is shown here:

```
require(JModuleHelper::getLayoutPath('mod_littlecontact',
        'default_tmpl'));
```

The first parameter is the module name, and the second parameter is the template name. Just remember three things:

1. If there's no second parameter, the template loaded will be the one named `default.php`.

> Note that we are using `default_tmpl.php`, so we need to pass it as the second parameter.

2. Templates need to be in the `tmpl` folder.

3. We don't need to put the `.php` extension, but only the file name, as the extension is PHP by default. If we were using another extension, such as `.php5`, then it would be necessary to place it.

With all this in place we need to make one little change to our `default_tmpl.php` file. We need to add a hidden file to our form, just after the form declaration:

```
<form action="index.php" method="post" id="sc_form">
    <input type="hidden" name="form_send" value="send" />
```

This will send the `form_send` variable that we have been talking about with a value of `"send"`. Then the switch will load our `sendok_tmpl.php` template instead of our `default_tmpl.php` one.

Go try it out! Now our module is fully functional—well, it doesn't send an e-mail, but it behaves as if it does.

Once you have given it a try, you can continue. We are now going to send an e-mail. We will place the necessary code inside the `mod_littlecontact.php` file's `switch` sentence. It will be placed exactly in the `send` case:

```
        case 'send':

            $your_name = JRequest::getVar('your_name', 'No name');
            $your_question = JRequest::getVar('your_question',
                'No question');

            $mail =& JFactory::getMailer();
```

```
$mail->setSender('demo@sender.com', 'Wayofthewebninja');
$mail->setSubject('Contact from our site');
$mail->addRecipient('demo@recipient.com');

$body = "Contact form send by user<br/>";
$body.= "------------------------<br/>";
$body.= "Username: ".$your_name."<br/>";
$body.= "Question: ".$your_question."<br/>";

$mail->setBody($body);
$mail->IsHTML(true);

$send =& $mail->Send();
if ( $send !== true ) {
    echo 'Error sending email: ' . $send->message;
}

require(JModuleHelper::getLayoutPath('mod_littlecontact',
        'sendok_tmpl'));
break;
```

This code is quite easy to understand; let's take a look together. First we take the variables sent by the form:

```
$your_name = JRequest::getVar('your_name', 'No name');
$your_question = JRequest::getVar('your_question',
    'No question');
```

Our next step is to initialize the mailer:

```
$mail =& JFactory::getMailer();
```

Set the sender, as follows:

```
$mail->setSender('demo@sender.com', 'Wayofthewebninja');
```

Now, write the subject:

```
$mail->setSubject('Contact from our site');
```

And, finally, add the recipient:

```
$mail->addRecipient('demo@recipient.com');
```

Then we prepare the content for our message, as follows:

```
$body = "Contact form send by user<br/>";
$body.= "------------------------<br/>";
$body.= "Username: ".$your_name."<br/>";
$body.= "Question: ".$your_question."<br/>";

$mail->setBody($body);
$mail->IsHTML(true);
```

Note that if you don't want to send the message as HTML, and instead you want to send it as plain text, don't set the IsHTML value. And try to send the message, showing errors if any occur, as follows:

```
$send =& $mail->Send();
if ( $send !== true ) {
    echo 'Error sending email: ' . $send->message;
}
```

That's it. Now when we send the form, an e-mail will also be sent. Of course, this is very basic; you can read more about sending e-mails with Joomla! at the following link:

http://docs.joomla.org/How_to_send_email_from_components

Or you could also read the book "Mastering Joomla! 1.5", available from Packt. Each one of these is a good option for learning more.

Now we will place this e-mail code in another file, just to organize it a bit. We will create a helper file, this way our mod_littlecontact.php won't be crowded. This will work in a similar fashion to our template files.

This file will be placed in modules/mod_littlecontact and will be named helper.php. For now only create the file; we will work with it shortly.

But before doing so, we are going to add this file to our mod_littlecontact.xml file, just to ensure that we don't forget about it:

```
<filename>helper.php</filename>
```

The content of the helper.php will be as follows:

```
<?php
defined('_JEXEC') or die('Direct Access to this location is not
allowed.');

class ModLittleContactHelper{
```

```
    public function SendMail($your_name, $your_question){

        $mail =& JFactory::getMailer();
        $mail->setSender('josemanises@gmail.com',
                'Wayofthewebninja');
        $mail->setSubject('Contact from our site');
        $mail->addRecipient('josemanises@gmail.com');

        $body = "Contact form send by user<br/>";
        $body.= "-----------------------<br/>";
        $body.= "Username: ".$your_name."<br/>";
        $body.= "Question: ".$your_question."<br/>";

        $mail->setBody($body);
        $mail->IsHTML(true);

        $send =& $mail->Send();

        return $send;

    }
}
?>
```

After taking a look at this code, you will notice that it's our old, small piece of code that sent the form. It has been placed inside a method called `SendMail`, which takes two parameters. And everything is placed inside a class called `ModLittleContactHelper`.

We could have given any name we liked to this class and method, but these names look fine. And now that our helper file is ready, we are going to make good use of it.

For this we are going to return to the `mod_littlecontact.php` file. I'm going to place it in full here, so that we can take a detailed look at it:

```
<?php
defined('_JEXEC') or die('Direct Access to this location is not
allowed.');

require_once(dirname(__FILE__).DS.'helper.php');

JHTML::stylesheet('styles.css','modules/mod_littlecontact/css/');

$form_send = JRequest::getVar('form_send', 'notsend');
```

```
switch($form_send){

    case 'send':

        $your_name = JRequest::getVar('your_name', 'No name');
        $your_question = JRequest::getVar('your_question',
            'No question');

        $send = ModLittleContactHelper::SendMail($your_name,
                $your_question);

        if ( $send !== true ) {
            echo 'Error sending email: ' . $send->message;
        }

        require(JModuleHelper::getLayoutPath('mod_littlecontact',
                'sendok_tmpl'));
        break;

    default:
        require(JModuleHelper::getLayoutPath('mod_littlecontact',
                'default_tmpl'));

}

?>
```

The first difference is in the following line:

```
require_once(dirname(__FILE__).DS.'helper.php');
```

With this line we include our helper file. Our next step is to make use of it by calling the method that we have just created, as follows:

```
$send = ModLittleContactHelper::SendMail($your_name, $your_question);
```

We also save the result to the $send variable so that we can check later if the e-mail has been sent.

We are done! Well at least in a very simple way. Sure we could do lots of things to enhance this little module, but we are going to concentrate on only two of them: sending the mail without needing to reload the page, and checking some required fields. Keep reading!

Making a better form using JavaScript

In this part of the chapter we are going to add some new features to our little module. These features are intended to make a better form, such as avoiding a full page reload by sending the form using AJAX or checking that some text has been introduced before sending it. All these are good features, though not every form needs to make use of these features. It's up to us to decide when to implement them.

But enough chat for now, work is awaiting us!

Send the form using jQuery AJAX

This is not going to be as hard as it may first seem, thanks to the powerful jQuery features. What steps do we need to take to achieve AJAX form sending? First, open our `default_tmpl.php` file. Here we are going to add an ID to our button, and change it a bit, from this:

```
<input type="submit" name="send" value="Send" class="sc_button"/>
```

to this:

```
<input type="button" name="send" value="Send" class="sc_button"
id="send_button"/>
```

Apart from adding the ID, we change its type from `submit` to `button`. And with this our form is prepared. We need a new file, a `js` one this time, to keep things organized. So we are going to create a `js` folder, and place a `littlecontact.js` file in it, and we will have the following path:

```
modules/mod_littlecontact/js/littlecontact.js
```

As always, we will also include this file in the `mod_littlecontact.xml` file, like this:

```
<filename>js/littlecontact.js</filename>
```

Before adding our code to the `littlecontact.js` file, we are going to add it to the header section of our site. We will do this in the `mod_littlecontact.php` file, as follows:

```
require_once(dirname(__FILE__).DS.'helper.php');

$document =& JFactory::getDocument();

$document->addScript(JURI::root(true).'modules'.DS.'
        mod_littlecontact'.DS.'js'.DS.'littlecontact.js');

JHTML::stylesheet('styles.css','modules/mod_littlecontact/css/');
```

I've highlighted the changes we need to make; first we get an instance to the global document object. Then we use the addScript method to add our script file to the header section.

We use JURI::root(true) to create a correct path. So now in our header, if we check the source code, we will see:

```
<script type="text/javascript" src="/modules/mod_littlecontact/js/
littlecontact.js"></script>
```

If instead of using JURI::root(true), we would have used JURI::root() our source code would look like the following:

```
<script type="text/javascript" src="http://wayofthewebninja.com/
 modules/mod_littlecontact/js/littlecontact.js"></script>
```

 You can find more information about the JURI::root method at:

http://docs.joomla.org/JURI/root

We are now ready to start working on our littlecontact.js file:

```
jQuery(document).ready(function($){
    $('#send_button').click(function() {
        $.post("index.php", $("#sc_form").serialize());
    });
});
```

It is a little piece of code, let's take a look at it. First we use the ready function, so all of our code is executed when the DOM is ready:

```
jQuery(document).ready(function($){
```

Then we add the click method to the #send_button button. This method will have a function inside with some more code. This time we are using the post method:

```
$.post("index.php", $("#sc_form").serialize());
```

The post method will send a request to a page, defined in the first parameter, using the HTTP post request method.

In the second parameter we can find the data we are sending to the page. We could pass an array with some data, but instead we are using the serialize method on our form, with ID sc_form.

The `serialize` method will read our form, and prepare a string for sending the data.

And that's all; our form will be sent, without our visitors even noticing. Go ahead and try it! Also, you could take a look to the following two pages:

- `http://api.jquery.com/jQuery.post/`
- `http://api.jquery.com/serialize/`

Here you can find some good information about these two functions. After you have taken a look at these pages, come back here, and we will continue.

Well, sending the form without page reloading is OK, we will save our visitors some time. But we need our visitors to notice that something is happening and most important, that the message has been sent.

We will now work on these two things. First of all we are going to place a message, so our readers will know that the form is being sent. This is going to be quite easy too.

First we are going to add some markup to our `default_tmpl.php`, as follows:

```php
<?php
defined('_JEXEC') or die('Direct Access to this location is not
allowed.');
?>
<div id="littlecontact">
    .
    .
    .


    <div id="sending_message" class="hidden_div">
        <br/><br/><br/>
       <h1>Your message is being sent, <br/>wait a bit.</h1>
    </div>

    <div id="message_sent" class="hidden_div">
        <br/><br/><br/>
       <h1>Your message has been sent.
          <br/>Thanks for contacting us.</h1>
       <br/><br/><br/>
       <a href="index.php" class="message_link"
         id="message_back">Back to the form</a>
    </div>
</div>
```

We have added two DIVs here: sending_message and message_sent. These two will help us show some messages to our visitors. With the messages prepared, we need some CSS styles, and we will define these in our module's styles.css file:

```
#littlecontact{
    position: relative;
}

#sending_message, #message_sent{
    height: 235px;
    width: 284px;
    position: absolute;
    z-index: 100;
    background-color: #5B5751;
    top: 0;
    text-align: center;
}

.hidden_div{
    visibility: hidden;
    display: none;
}

.show_div{
    visibility: visible;
    display: block;
}

a.message_link:link, a.message_link:visited{
    color: #ffffff;
    text-decoration: none;
}

a.message_link:hover{
    text-decoration: underline;
}
```

Don't worry about writing all this code; you can find it in the code bundle, so copy it from there. Going back to the code, these are just simple CSS styles, and some of the most important ones are the hidden_div and show_div classes. These will be used to show or hide the messages.

Ready to go to the JavaScript code? We will now return to our `littlecontact.js` file and modify it a bit:

```
jQuery(document).ready(function($){
    $('#send_button').click(function() {
        $.post("index.php", $("#sc_form").serialize(), show_ok());

        $("#sending_message").removeClass("hidden_div");
    });

    $("#message_back").click(function(e){
        e.preventDefault();
        $("#message_sent").addClass("hidden_div");
        $("#sending_message").addClass("hidden_div");
    });

    function show_ok(){
        $("#sending_message").addClass("hidden_div");
        $("#message_sent").removeClass("hidden_div");

        $("input:text").val('');
        $("textarea").val('');
    }
});
```

Seems a lot? Don't worry, we will take a step-by-step look at it. If we look at our previously added `click` function, we can see a new line, as follows:

```
$("#sending_message").removeClass("hidden_div");
```

This will search for our `sending_message` DIV, and remove the `hidden_div` class. This way the DIV will be visible, and we will see a screen similar to the following screenshot:

A nice message tells our visitors that the e-mail is being sent just at the moment. But we don't do only that. If we take a closer look at our previous post method, we will see some changes, as follows:

```
$.post("index.php", $("#sc_form").serialize(), show_ok());
```

A new third parameter! This is a callback function, which will be executed when the request succeeds and our e-mail has been sent. But what is inside this `show_ok` function? Its contents are as follows:

```
function show_ok(){
        $("#sending_message").addClass("hidden_div");
        $("#message_sent").removeClass("hidden_div");

        $("input:text").val('');
        $("textarea").val('');
    }
```

First we add the `hidden_div` class to the `sending_message`, so this sending message is not seen any more. But instead we remove the `hidden_div` class of our `message_sent` DIV, so our visitors will see this new message:

But we are also emptying our inputs, text inputs, and `textarea` fields:

```
        $("input:text").val('');
        $("textarea").val('');
```

So when visitors return to the form they are presented with a fresh one, just in case they have forgotten something and want to send a new e-mail. Hey who knows!

Our last step is to enable a back link, so that the readers can return to the form:

```
$("#message_back").click(function(e){
    e.preventDefault();
    $("#message_sent").addClass("hidden_div");
    $("#sending_message").addClass("hidden_div");
});
```

First we target the link using its ID, and then we bind a `click` function to it. The next step is to prevent the default event for the link. This is why the link won't behave as a link, and won't try to load a page. This is why we are not going to load or reload a page, instead we will continue with our code, hiding both DIVs, so the form is visible again.

That's it! It has not been that hard, has it? Now, it would be a great moment to take a look at the code bundle, see the code, read it, and try it by yourself. Or alternatively, keep reading a bit more if you want!

Tips and tricks

Look at the site `http://www.ajaxload.info/`. There you will be able to generate some loader GIF images. These will act as the typical clock mouse, telling the users that something is happening. Maybe you would like to use that instead of only using text. Give it a try!

Validating form fields using jQuery—why validate?

Ah! validating forms, so entertaining. It's just the kind of task everyone always wants to do. Well, maybe a bit less than others. But it's something that needs to be done. Why? Just to ensure that we are receiving the proper data, or even that we are receiving data.

Ideally we would use JavaScript validation on the client side, and PHP validation on the server side. Server-side validation is essential, so a user turning off JavaScript still gets his/her contents validated. JavaScript validation will save us the effort of having to send all the data to the server, and then come back with the errors.

We are going to use a bit of JavaScript to try to validate our form. This process is going to be quite simple too, as our form is very small.

We will be doing all of our work in our `littlecontact.js` file. Remember our `$('#send_button').click` function? It looked like this:

```
$('#send_button').click(function() {
    $.post("index.php", $("#sc_form").serialize(), show_ok());

    $("#sending_message").removeClass("hidden_div");
});
```

Now with some modifications, it will be more or less as follows:

```
$('#send_button').click(function() {
    //First we do some validation,
    //just to know that we have some data
    alerts = '';
    if($("input[name=your_name]").val() == ''){
        alerts += "we need your name\n";
    }
    if($("textarea[name=your_question]").val().length < 5){
        alerts += "We need a message of at least 5 characters
                    length\n";
    }

    if(alerts != ''){
        alert(alerts);
    }else{
        $.post("index.php", $("#sc_form").serialize(),
                show_ok());
        $("#sending_message").removeClass("hidden_div");
    }
});
```

First, we define a new variable, to put all the messages in:

```
alerts = '';
```

Then we check our form fields (first the input text):

```
if($("input[name=your_name]").val() == '')
```

As you can see, with jQuery we can select the input with a `name` equal to `your_name` and check if its value is empty. The `textarea` check is very similar:

```
if($("textarea[name=your_question]").val().length < 5
```

But we are also checking if the length of the value is greater than five. After each one of these validations, if failed, we add a message to the `alerts` variable. Later, we will check if that variable is not empty. If it's not empty, it would mean that some of the checks have failed, and then we show the alerts to our visitors:

```
alert(alerts);
```

This will raise a typical alert message, much like the following screenshot:

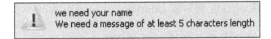

Informative, but not really nice. But thinking about it, we already have the jQuery UI library available, thanks to our SC jQuery Joomla! plugin. Why not use that plugin to show a better message? Let's do it. First we need to make some changes in the `default_tmpl.php` file:

```
<div id="alerts" title="Errors found in the form"
  style="display: none;"></div>
```

We have added a new DIV, with an ID equal to `alerts`, and with an informative `title`. Now that our markup is ready, some changes are also necessary in our `littlecontact.js` JavaScript file.

For example, we are going to change our alert messages from the following:

```
alerts += "- We need your name\n";
  .
  .
  .
alerts += "- We need a message of at least 5 characters length\n";
```

To the following:

```
alerts += "- We need your name<br/>";
  .
  .
  .
alerts += "- We need a message of at least 5 chapters length<br/>";
```

Why are we doing this? It is because we will show HTML in our dialog, instead of just text. How are we going to show the dialog? Quite easily, by changing the following line:

```
alert(alerts);
```

To this:

```
$("#alerts").html(alerts).dialog();
```

What are we doing here? First, we select our newly created DIV, with ID `alerts`, and then we use the `html` method, passing the variable `alerts` as its parameter. This will fill our DIV with the content of the `alerts` variable.

Nested in it we will find the `dialog` method. This is a jQuery UI method that will create a dialog box, as we can see in the following screenshot:

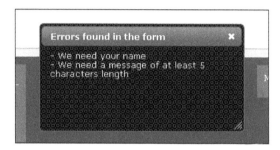

Better than our previous alert message, isn't it? Also notice that this dialog is matching the style of all our jQuery UI elements, like the login dialog and the tabs module. If we were to change the style in the SC jQuery Joomla! plugin, the style of the dialog will also change.

 If you want to know more about the jQuery UI dialog method, check the following page:

`http://jqueryui.com/demos/dialog/`

Well that's it for now. This is just a small example; now don't you think it would be great to give it a try? Just open the code bundle and check it!

Warning

Much work should be added to this example to make a real world application of it, such as adding better security and error support.

An easy to add security measure would be to use the `JMailHelper` class:

`http://api.joomla.org/Joomla-Framework/Mail/JMailHelper.html`

This class can help us check if we are using a proper e-mail, or check that no headers have been injected in the subject, body, and so on.

For example, in our module, if we want to check that no headers have been injected in our body, we could do it like this. The following excerpt is from the `modules/mod_littlecontact/helper.php` file:

```
jimport('joomla.mail.helper');

$body = JMailHelper::cleanText($body);

$mail->setBody($body);
```

First we import the helper class, then we use the `cleanText` method to check our `$body` variable. Easy, isn't it? Just check the previous URL, you will see some useful methods to use.

What could you check?

One interesting way in which you could enhance this little module is by using a curious technique called Honeypot Captcha. It is very easy to implement and use, just search for it.

Another way that might be more appropriate for a bigger project, would be to use a jQuery form validation plugin, just like the following:

- `http://plugins.jquery.com/project/SimpleValidator`
- `http://plugins.jquery.com/project/Salid`
- `http://plugins.jquery.com/project/ec_jq_form_validator`
- `http://plugins.jquery.com/project/jquery-validator`

This is just to name some of them, but there are many more good ones.

What to do next? Packing and installing the module

Packing is the end part of our little module project. After packing the module, we will be able to use our module in every project very easily. This process is quite easy; just ZIP all the files and folders inside our `modules/mod_littlecontact` folder, so we will have the following structure:

```
mod_littlecontact.zip
-   css
-   styles.css
-   js
```

- littlecontact.js
- tmpl
- default_tmpl.php
- sendok_tmpl.php
- helper.php
- index.html
- mod_littlecontact.php
- mod_littlecontact.xml

But before trying to install our module, we will uninstall our previous installation, so that we can check if the installation process has gone OK.

Go to the administrator page, then **Extensions | Install/Uninstall | Modules**, and on that screen look for **mod_littlecontact**. Select it and click on the **Uninstall** button.

Well we have just uninstalled the module, so we can now install it again with our new ZIP file. Go to **Extensions | Install/Uninstall**, select the file, and click on the **Upload File & Install** button.

And that's all; this module will be available for us every time we need it.

Having problems with the installation? If the installation seems to be unable to complete, you could try the following:

- Check your XML file, to ensure it's correct.
- Check your FTP configuration, to ensure it's correct. This can be done on **Site | Global Configuration | Server.**
- Disable FTP in the previous screen.
- Instead of using the ZIP compression format, compress to tar.gzip.
- Give 777 permissions to the modules folder.
- Try to upload the module and install using install from URL or from directory.

Hopefully, one of these options will work and solve any possible problems.

Summary

Well I hope you have really enjoyed this chapter. We have covered some interesting topics here, such as the basics of module creation, building our little contact module, and then enhancing it with AJAX and some other nice features.

Building a basic module, and then enhancing it with the features we want, or need, is an easy task. Try not to start with something over complicated; realistic objectives are always more achievable.

In the next chapter, we are going to concentrate on the backend part, the administrator. Though visitors usually don't get to see that part, it's really important, and will make our components and modules look more professional. Let's continue then!

8

Building Complete Solutions, Modules, and Components

"Mixing modules and components for great results"

In the previous chapter, we worked on a tiny module, focusing our efforts only on the frontend. This time, we are going to create a simple component too. This way we will be able to work in the backend part and insert data into the database. But don't worry, this is going to be very simple—just the basics so that we have some data inserted—and then we will use a module to show it on the frontend.

For the example in this chapter, we are going to build a news rotator module. Although it is going to be quite simple on the frontend, we will be adding some interesting features in the admin panel.

In this chapter, we will be covering the following topics:

- Working on our news rotator module
- Creating the component base
- How Joomla! helps us in working with the database
- Modifying our installer to create our table
- Coding a basic admin zone
- Inserting, editing, and deleting records in our admin zone
- Showing the data in our module
- Adding jQuery to our module and refreshing data using JavaScript

At the end of the chapter, we will have created a fully featured module and component solution, and the best part of all is that you will be able to use this knowledge in all of your projects.

So, are you ready? Let's get started.

Working with the news rotator module

The basics of our module are going to be mostly the same as in our previous module. In fact, I've prepared a basic module installation with only the basic files. You can find it in the code bundle, and it is called `mod_tinynews.tar.gz`.

As always, our first step will be to install this file. But before continuing, and just to make sure we don't forget about it, we will go to the administrator screen, navigate to **Extensions | Plugin Manager** and open **System - SC jQuery plugin**.

Make sure that the plugin is also enabled for the backend, as we can see in the following screenshot:

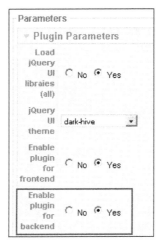

We have been using this plugin in the book, mostly for the frontend of our site. However, we can also use it in the backend for our module's admin zone. Enabling the plugin for the backend will let us use the power of jQuery on the administrator screen.

> If you don't have the SC jQuery plugin and don't want to use it, you can add the jQuery library to the administrator template. Take a look at the `administrator/templates` folder. For example, I'm using the khepri template. Inside, we can find a `js` folder where we can place the jQuery library. Then by opening the `index.php` file of the template, we can add it as follows:
>
> ```
> <script type="text/javascript" src="templates/<?php
> echo $this->template ?>/js/jquery.js"></script>
> ```
>
> And that's all we need to do to enable the jQuery library on our administrator screen.

Now that we have ensured we will have jQuery in our administrator backend, we are going to check if the new module we have installed is listed. Go to the administrator screen, then to **Extensions | Module Manager**, and click on **Tiny News**.

Here we can see the basic details and, most importantly, the module position. This time, we are going to use the **module_6** position of our template, as shown in the following screenshot:

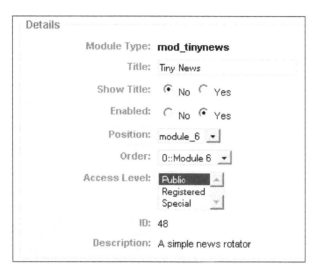

Good, now we have our module published in the position we want—though in the frontend we won't see anything, at least for now. To check if the module is working, we are going to make it show something. Open the `modules/mod_tinynews/mod_tinynews.php` file. We are going to add the highlighted line in the following code snippet:

```
require_once(dirname(__FILE__).DS.'helper.php');
require(JModuleHelper::getLayoutPath('mod_tinynews','default_tmpl'));
```

And then we are also going to perform some tiny changes in the template file located at `modules/mod_tinynews/tmpl/default_tmpl.php`. We will add the following code:

```
<div id-"tinynews">
  <?php echo "This is working"; ?>
</div>
```

Once that's done, our module will show the **This is working** message in our template's module position. Okay, then we will create the component part; don't worry, it's going to be easy.

Creating the component base

Let's start with the basics, step by step. We are going to work a bit on the frontend of our component. I think it will be easier to start in the frontend part. We are going to create a `com_tinynews` folder inside our `components` folder. Inside this folder, create a `tinynews.php` file with the following content:

```php
<?php
defined( '_JEXEC' ) or die( 'Restricted access' );

require_once( JPATH_COMPONENT.DS.'controller.php' );

$controller   = new TinynewsController();

$controller->execute($task = null);
```

Again, here we are using the `_JEXEC` constant to check if our file is being called by Joomla!. Then we require the `controller.php` file, which we haven't created yet.

The `JPATH_COMPONENT` constant defines the path to our component, and the `DS` constant defines the directory separator, be it / or \, depending on the system.

After we create an instance of the controller class, we call the `execute` method. We can pass a parameter here, but as the `$task` variable is not defined, a null value will be used instead.

Now our `tinynews.php` file is done, we will use it as a central point for our component. Most of the times that Joomla! calls the component, it will in fact be calling this file. But what about our controller file? We need to create it in `components/com_tinynews/` and call it `controller.php`. Let's have a look at its content:

```php
<?php
defined( '_JEXEC' ) or die( 'Restricted access' );

jimport('joomla.application.component.controller');

class TinynewsController extends JController{

    function display(){
        parent::display();
    }

}
```

Again, you can see that our well-known _JEXEC line is in the beginning. We then use
jimport in order to include the /libraries/joomla/application/component/
controller.php file, which has the JController class. Our own class will extend
this file.

 Note that jimport has replaced dots "." to "/" or "\" as necessary, and
added the .php extension to the end, thus loading the correct file.

After we have imported the file, we define our own class, TinynewsController,
which extends the JController class. This way we will have all the JController
methods available to us.

We can also see a display method. By default, this method will be called when no
other method is. Remember the following controller:

```
$controller->execute($task = null);
```

In it, we didn't mention which method to call, so the display method will be
called. Now we need a view file. For example, we are going to create a file called
components/com_tinynews/views/tinynews/view.html.php. Its content is
as follows:

```
<?php
defined( '_JEXEC' ) or die( 'Restricted access' );

jimport( 'joomla.application.component.view');

class TinynewsViewTinynews extends JView{

    function display(){

        $name = "Tinynews component!";
        $this->assignRef( 'name', $name );

        parent::display();
    }
}
```

Our first step, as always, is to check the _JEXEC constant. Then we import the view
class, from which our class TinynewsViewTinynews will be extended. Here we have
a display function with some code in it—but not too much. We have a $name variable
definition, after which we use the assignRef method to assign a new name variable
with the value of $name.

Assigning the variable will make it available in the template. So what do we need now? Yes, you have guessed it, a template. Create it in `components/com_tinynews/views/tinynews/tmpl/default.php`. Wow, that's quite a long path! However, let's put some content into this file:

```php
<?php defined('_JEXEC') or die('Restricted access'); ?>

<h1><?php echo $this->name; ?></h1>
```

Very little is done here; we are only showing our variable. And well, that's all we need for now. How can we check if all this is working? Quite easily. Imagine our site is called `wayofthewebninja.com`; if we wanted to load our component, we would use the following URL:

`http://wayofthewebninja.com/index.php?option=com_tinynews.`

We use the `option` variable to indicate which component needs to be loaded. This time it will be our component `com_tinynews`. Good, if all goes okay, we will see something similar to the following screenshot:

It's working! It has been quite easy, hasn't it? Well, maybe you have some questions in mind. Don't worry; we will be seeing most of the details step by step. Let's summarize all this a bit:

- First we created a `tinynews.php` file. This file will be an entry point to our component. All calls will be made to this file.

- Next we have a `controller.php` file, most of the logic lies here.

- Next we have a `view.html.php` file to prepare all what is about to be shown to our site visitors.

- Also, we have a `default.php` file, a template that will organize and show the data prepared in our view.

What is important to note here is the naming convention. If we don't name our classes the correct way, things won't work. Take for example, our controller. Our controller class is called:

```
class TinynewsController
```

Our component name ends with `Controller`, as follows:

```
class ComponentnameController
```

This is quite straightforward, but what about the view? This is a bit more difficult, as shown next:

```
class TinynewsViewTinynews
```

First we have our component name, then `View`, and then our view's name. So we have the following format:

```
class ComponentnameViewviewname
```

By default, our controller loads the view whose name is equal to the component name. How can we define another view to load? Quite easily; in our controller, we will add a `$_name` variable, indicating the view name, as follows:

```
class TinynewsController extends JController{

  var $_name='viewtoload';

    function display(){
        parent::display();
    }
}
```

Now that things are a bit better explained, or at least I hope so! We will continue with this example. This way we will get a better understanding of how things work.

XML installer file

This moment would be a great time to start creating our XML installer file. We are going to create it in the `components/com_tinynews` folder, and we will call it `tinynews.xml`. Let's have a look at its content:

```
<?xml version="1.0" encoding="utf-8"?>
<install type="component" version="1.5.0">
  <name>Tinynews</name>
  <creationDate>2010-03-07</creationDate>
  <author>Jose Argudo</author>
  <authorEmail>jose@joseargudo.com</authorEmail>
```

```
<authorUrl>http://www.joseargudo.com</authorUrl>
<copyright>Jose Argudo Blanco.</copyright>
<license>GPL 2.0</license>
<version>1.0</version>
<description>Component Tinynews</description>

<files folder="site">
<filename>controller.php</filename>
<filename>tinynews.php</filename>
<filename>index.html</filename>
<filename>views/index.html</filename>
<filename>views/tinynews/index.html</filename>
<filename>views/tinynews/view.html.php</filename>
<filename>views/tinynews/tmpl/default.php</filename>
<filename>views/tinynews/tmpl/index.html</filename>
</files>

<administration>

<menu>Component Tinynews</menu>

<files folder="admin">
 <filename>tinynews.php</filename>
 <filename>index.html</filename>
</files>

</administration>
</install>
```

As you can see, it is much like the XML we generated for our module. But then we have the `files` section. For example, take a look at the first line:

```
<files folder="site">
```

Here we are indicating to our installer that all the files between the `<files></files>` tag can be found inside a folder called `site`. Later, in the `administration` part, we indicate that we have a folder called `admin`, and also a `menu` tag. The name inside this will be the name that will appear in the **Components** menu of our administrator.

Don't worry about the `tinynews.php` inside the `admin` part, we will use that later.

It's quite a complex structure, so why don't you take a look into it for real? In the code bundle for Chapter 8, there's a folder called com_tinynews_ step_1. Inside this folder, you will see a file called com_tinynews. tar.gz. You can uncompress it to see the structure of the component.

And that's all! As we continue working, you will get a better understanding of all these concepts.

Why are so many files necessary?

Some of you who know about the MVC pattern will already be aware about why we need all these files.

But maybe some of you don't really know the reason behind this file division. I will try to explain it quickly so that all of us can work at the same level.

As I've said, Joomla! uses a development pattern called MVC. In a simplistic way, while developing the first step of our component, we have created several files. Each one of these files can be placed in one of these categories:

- **Model** — is used to work with data, be it retrieving data from a database, an XML file, or any other source of data. We use models to get the data. Our next step will be to build a model, but that will come in a moment.

- **View** — is the file that renders the information to our visitors. Here we should see very little code, mostly we will show data to our visitors. No manipulation is required.

- **Controller** — is where all the programming logic takes place. Controllers call models to get the data and then they pass this data to views. Finally, this data is rendered by the views.

The usual process would be as follows:

1. First we have the entry point. All requests will be made through this file. In our case, this was the `tinynews.php` file. This file is in charge of loading the necessary controller.

2. `controller.php` is our next step. Our entry point will load a controller and then use some methods from it.

3. Then the controller, if necessary, can load a model or, as we have seen in our example, go directly and load a view.

4. A view will prepare the data to be shown and, if necessary, use any templates necessary.

5. And finally, our result is rendered on the visitor's machine.

It's easier than it seems the first time you see it. By the end of the chapter, you will be used to this. Well, can you guess what our next step is? It's building a model!

Building our first model

As we have seen before, models are used to work with data, be it from a database or any other source. The models are where we will place our SQL queries and get the results that will be passed to the controllers.

Models will be placed in their own folder, `components/com_tinynews/models`, so first create this `models` folder. Inside this folder, we will create a file called `tinynews.php`, which will contain the following code:

```php
<?php

defined( '_JEXEC' ) or die( 'Restricted access' );

jimport( 'joomla.application.component.model' );

class TinynewsModelTinynews extends JModel{

    function getallnews(){

        $news[1] = "This is the title for the first news";
        $news[2] = "This is the content for the first news";
        $news[3] = "This is the title for the second news";
        $news[4] = "This is the content for the second news";

        return $news;
    }
}
```

There isn't much for now, but as we have not yet prepared a database, we need to put some demo data, and this is the best place.

The naming convention is very similar to what we have seen earlier. First is the name of the component, then the word `Model`, and then the name of the model, as follows:

```
Componentname**Model**Modelname
```

Also, note that we are using `jimport` again, but this time to import the Joomla! model class. So, all its methods will be available for us to use. Just after that we define the `getallnews` method and put some demo data there in an array.

After we have created our model, we are ready to use it with some tiny changes to our view. If you remember, in our view (excerpt is taken from `components/com_tinynews/views/tinynews/view.html.php`), we had the following:

```
class TinynewsViewTinynews extends JView{

    function display(){

        $name = "Tinynews component!";
        $this->assignRef( 'name', $name );
```

We need to change this code a bit so that we can use our newly created model, as follows:

```
        $model =& $this->getModel();
        $news = $model->getallnews();
        $this->assignRef('news', $news);
```

First of all, we get the model so that we can use it. By default, our view will load the model that shares the same name, which is `Tinynews`. In any other case, we will need to put the name of the model we want to load.

Next, we call the `getallnews` method from our model and place the results in a variable. These results will be passed to the template later, using the `assignRef` method.

As you may be guessing, we now need to work on our template, so these changes take effect. Open the `components/com_tinynews/views/tinynews/tmpl/default.php` file, and change all its content to the following:

```
<?php

defined('_JEXEC') or die('Restricted access');

foreach($this->news as $new){

    echo "<p>".$new."</p><br/><br/>";

}

?>
```

In our template we use a simple `foreach` loop in order to show all elements of our array, and that's all. So, if we now try to go to `http://www.yoursite.com/index.php?option=com_tinynews`, we will see something similar to the following screenshot:

Well, we are still far away from our final result, but our example component is getting more interesting. Now, before continuing, we are going to update our XML file, as shown in the highlighted code:

```
<files folder="site">
...
   <filename>models/index.html</filename>
   <filename>models/tinynews.php</filename>
</files>
```

> Having problems? Why don't you take a look at the code bundle? There is a folder called `com_tinynews_step_2` with a file inside called `com_tinynews.tar.gz` that contains all the code so far.

How Joomla! helps us work with the database

At this point we can start thinking about the database. Without that our component wouldn't be of much use. As you will see, Joomla!'s database class will be more helpful this time. For now, we are going to create the table that we are going to use. The query is as follows:

```
CREATE TABLE `jos_tinynews` (
`id` INT NOT NULL AUTO_INCREMENT PRIMARY KEY ,
```

```
`title` VARCHAR( 255 ) NOT NULL ,
`text` TEXT NOT NULL
)
```

As we can see, we have placed the prefix `jos_` to our `tinynews` table name. That's the prefix that we usually use, but if you are using another prefix, place it there. Once we have the table created, we can start experimenting with it. The other two fields are `title` and `text`. Later we will be adding some more fields, but these will be okay for now.

We are going to see some basic examples of work, such as:

- Inserting data into our table
- Editing data from our table
- Deleting data
- And finally, selecting data

Ready? Let's get started.

Inserting data

This can be done in more than one way; we will be checking some of the methods available, so you can decide later which one to use. Though it's not so usual, we are only going to work with the following two files:

- Our view — `components/com_tinynews/views/tinynews/view.html.php`
- Our model — `components/com_tinynews/models/tinynews.php`

That's not the usual way of doing things, but for a demonstration it will be enough. We will start working on the model, so open the model file. We are going to add a new method called `insertdata` to it, as follows:

```php
function insertdata($title = "default", $text = "default"){

    $database =& JFactory::getDBO();

    $news = new stdClass;
    $news->id = NULL;
    $news->title = $title;
    $news->text = $text;

    if (!$database->insertObject( '#__tinynews', $news, 'id' )) {
        echo $database->stderr();
```

```
        return false;
    }
    return $news->id;
}
```

With this tiny piece of code, we will have created our new method. This method receives two parameters, $title and $text. We are assigning a default value to these two, just in case no data is passed to the method.

Our next step is to create an instance of the database object so that all its methods are available to us. We do this with $database =& JFactory::getDBO();. After this is done, we are going to create an object. For this type of database insert, we are going to use the following object:

```
$news = new stdClass;
$news->id = NULL;
$news->title = $title;
$news->text = $text;
```

In order to create this object we are using the class stdClass. This is an empty class that comes with PHP. It has no methods or properties, so we can define it to our liking. After we have prepared our class with the values passed to our method, we will try to insert it and take care of any possible errors:

```
if (!$database->insertObject( '#__tinynews', $news, 'id' )) {
    echo $database->stderr();
    return false;
}
```

We use the insertObject method, and if things don't go well, we return false; otherwise we will return the last inserted ID with return $news->id;.

Once we have our method created in the model, we are going to make use of it in our view file. Open the components/com_tinynews/views/tinynews/view.html.php file and add the highlighted code to it:

```
function display(){

    $model =& $this->getModel();

    $news = $model->getallnews();
    $this->assignRef('news', $news);
```

```
$insertnews = $model->insertdata("Our first news inserted",
                    "This will be the text for our first news");
echo "<br/><br/>Our newly inserted news has id:
    ".$insertnews."<br/><br/>";

    parent::display();
}
```

First, we need to check if we are correctly loading our model using
`$model =& $this->getModel();`.

If the model has been loaded, we will be able to make use of its methods. In our
example, we will call our newly created `insertdata` method, passing some values
to it. We will also assign its returned value to the `$insertnews` variable.

This returned value will be then rendered to screen, showing the ID of the
inserted element. For example, if we try to load our site again by calling the
`http://wayofthewebninja.com/index.php?option=com_tinynews` URL,
we will see something similar to the following screenshot:

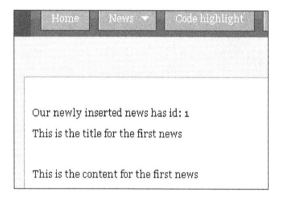

Note that we have used #__tinynews instead of jos_tinynews. Joomla!
will change #__ to jos_ or any other prefix that is being used in our
Joomla! installation. This way we can install our component in any Joomla!
installation without needing to change the prefix for each installation.

Now that we have successfully inserted our new record, we are going to see another way of doing it, just so you can decide which method you like best. We will be changing the insertdata method of our model, as follows:

```
function insertdata($title = "default", $text = "default"){

    $database =& JFactory::getDBO();

    $query = "INSERT INTO ".$database->nameQuote('#__tinynews').
    "(title, text) VALUES (".$database->quote($title).",".
    $database->quote($text).")";

    $database->setQuery($query);

      if (!$database->query()) {
        echo $database->stderr();
        return false;
      }

    return $database->insertid();
}
```

Though this is a bit different, we will have the same result. This time we are building the query in a more "classical" way. However, we are still using some Joomla! methods that will help us in our work. Take for example these two:

- `$database->nameQuote`
- `$database->quote`

These two methods are going to be very useful for us. The first method, nameQuote, will place backticks (` `) around our table name if we use MySQL. If we were using other database, Joomla! will place backticks or any other character that is necessary.

The quote method does something similar, but it's used for values instead of tables or field names. Not only will this method surround the values in quotes (' '), but it will also escape special characters that could harm our database, thus helping us prevent SQL injection attacks.

 Want to know more about SQL injection? You can start here: http://en.wikipedia.org/wiki/SQL_injection.

We have prepared our query and now we need to set it. We do that with `$database->setQuery($query);`. This sets the query for execution, but doesn't execute it. For that we need to use the `$database->query()` method.

We can check for errors much in the same way as in the first `insertdata` example. However, for taking the last inserted ID, we need to use the `$database->insertid();` method.

And that's all. Any of these two ways will help us in inserting data into the database. We can do this a few more times by just reloading that URL.

Come on! Do it three or four more times so that we have some data to work with. Our next step will be to update data, which will be quite similar.

Updating data

Updating our data will be necessary from time to time, and it will be quite similar to our latest insert example. Open the `components/com_tinynews/models/tinynews.php` file if you haven't opened it yet. We are going to remove our `insertdata` method and replace it with an `updatedata` method as follows:

```
function updatedata($id = "0", $title = "default", $text =
   "default"){

   $database =& JFactory::getDBO();

   $query = "UPDATE ".$database->nameQuote('#__tinynews').
   " SET ".$database->nameQuote('title').
"=".$database->quote($title).", ".$database->nameQuote('text').
"=".$database->quote($text)." WHERE ".$database->nameQuote('id').
"=".$database->quote($id);

   $database->setQuery($query);

   if (!$database->query()) {
     echo $database->stderr();
     return false;
   }

}
```

As you can see, the only thing that really changes here is the query. But it's not very different from every other update query we have seen in other occasions. Next, I will show you a delete query.

Deleting records

Again, we will be doing this in a similar way to what we could have been doing without Joomla!. Take a look at the `deletedata` method:

```
function deletedata($id = "0"){

$database =& JFactory::getDBO();

$query = "DELETE FROM ".$database->nameQuote('#__tinynews').
" WHERE ".$database->nameQuote('id')." = ".$database->quote($id);

  $database->setQuery($query);

  if (!$database->query()) {
    echo $database->stderr();
    return false;
  }

}
```

Not much to say here. Why don't we go to something more interesting such as reading data? Joomla! has some interesting methods for reading data. Let's get started with them!

Reading data

Reading data is going to be the most interesting part of our work with the database, mostly because here Joomla! has more methods to work with. For example, there is the `loadResult` method, which we will start with.

We will continue working on the following two files:

- **Our view**: `components/com_tinynews/views/tinynews/view.html.php`
- **Our model**: `components/com_tinynews/models/tinynews.php`

loadResult

This one is used to get just one value from our database, like a field from our table. Let's try it; we are going to create a `get_title` method in our model:

```
function get_title($id = 0){

$database =& JFactory::getDBO();

$query = "SELECT ".$database->nameQuote('title').
```

```
    "FROM ".$database->nameQuote('#__tinynews').
    " WHERE ".$database->nameQuote('id')." = ".$database->quote($id);

    $database->setQuery($query);

    $result = $database->loadResult();

    return $result;
}
```

This method will receive an ID, which will be used to retrieve the value we want from the database. Our first step, as always, is to get an instance of the database class. Then we prepare the query we are going to use to retrieve the title from the record with the ID equal to the one passed to the method.

The next step is to set the query with the setQuery method. Then only one thing still needs to be done—calling the loadResult method. This method, as many others we are about to see, automatically calls the query method so that we don't need to call the query method to execute the query. It will be automatically executed by the loadResult method.

Once that's done, we return the value. Take a look at the following highlighted code:

```
function display(){

    $model =& $this->getModel();

    $news = $model->getallnews();
    $this->assignRef('news', $news);

    $title = $model->get_title('1');
    echo $title."<br/><br/>";

    parent::display();
}
```

If we add the code to our view display method, we only need to load our usual http://wayofthewebninja.com/index.php?option=com_tinynews URL. A phrase like **Our first news inserted** will be shown on our screen. But what if we want more than just one value returned? Well, there are other methods for that, and we are about to see them. Take for example the loadObject method.

loadObject

The `loadObject` method will return a full record instead of a single value. We will see this better with an example. Let's modify the `get_title` method in our model. Call it `get_record` and modify its code as follows:

```
function get_record($id = 0){

    $database =& JFactory::getDBO();

    $query = "SELECT * FROM ".$database->nameQuote('#__tinynews').
    " WHERE ".$database->nameQuote('id')." = ".$database->quote($id);

    $database->setQuery($query);

    $result = $database->loadObject();

    return $result;
}
```

See, we have changed our `loadResult` method to our `loadObject` one, but mostly the method remains exactly as it is except for the query. We are returning all the fields now. So our model doesn't need many changes, but what about our view? We will change the `display` method of our view as follows:

```
$record = $model->get_record('1');
echo $record->id."<br/><br/>";
echo $record->title."<br/><br/>";
echo $record->text."<br/><br/>";
```

This will render something like this on our screen:

```
1

Our first news inserted

This will be the text for our first news
```

So the `loadObject` method has created an object, each field of the record being a property of the object. This is my favorite way of returning and working with a single record. But there are others, such as:

- `loadRow()` — works in mostly the same way, but instead of returning an object, returns an indexed array (so our previous example would work in a similar manner)

- `loadAssoc()` — is a method that can be used to return an associative array, instead of an indexed one

At this point, we have only seen the tip of the iceberg. The database class has many, many other methods, which we can use to fulfill all our needs. If you want to check them all, you can go to the following page:

```
http://docs.joomla.org/How_to_use_the_database_classes_in_your_script.
```

But before going there, stay with us, as we are going to see one last method, called loadObjectList.

loadObjectList

loadObjectList is probably one of the methods that we are going to use most of the time. It returns an array of objects. For this example, we will modify the getallnews method of our model. It will look as follows:

```
function getallnews(){

    $database =& JFactory::getDBO();

    $query = "SELECT * FROM ".
             $database->nameQuote('#__tinynews').";";

    $database->setQuery($query);

    $result = $database->loadObjectList();

    return $result;
}
```

Again, there aren't many changes here—only the loading method and the query. We have removed the WHERE part of the query, and so we get all the results from the table. The next thing we need to change is our view file, as follows:

```
function display(){

    $model =& $this->getModel();

    $news = $model->getallnews();
    $this->assignRef('news', $news);

    parent::display();
}
```

Not many changes here either, but then, this time we need to change our template `components\com_tinynews\views\tinynews\tmpl\default.php` file, as follows:

```php
<?php

defined('_JEXEC') or die('Restricted access');

foreach($this->news as $new){

   echo "<p><b>".$new->title."</b></p><br/><br/>";
   echo "<p>".$new->text."</p><br/><br/>";

}

?>
```

This code is almost self-explanatory; for each element of the `$this->news` array we create a new variable, `$new`. Each one of these variables will be an object, much like our `loadObject` example. This code will result in a screenshot as follows:

With all these methods, we will be able to insert, edit, delete, and retrieve data from our table. All this will not only be necessary when building the admin zone of our component, but also on the frontend of our module so that we can retrieve the data in order to show it to our site visitors.

Modifying our installer to create our table

When installing our component, we will need to create the necessary table. After all, we want to make things as automatic as possible and, unlike in modules, components are able to execute SQL queries during installation.

As there is the possibility of running queries during component installation, we are going to make use of this useful feature. In fact, it's quite easy. First we need to modify our `tinynews.xml` file, as follows:

```
...
</files>

<install>
 <sql>
   <file charset="utf8" driver="mysql">install.sql</file>
 </sql>
</install>
<uninstall>
 <sql>
   <file charset="utf8" driver="mysql">uninstall.sql</file>
 </sql>
</uninstall>

<administration>

 <menu>Component Tinynews</menu>

 <files folder="admin">
  <filename>tinynews.php</filename>
  <filename>index.html</filename>
  <filename>install.sql</filename>
  <filename>uninstall.sql</filename>
 </files>

</administration>
```

Here we have added some `install` and `uninstall` tags between our `<files>` and `<administration>` part. These tags will be in charge of executing the `install.sql` file when installing the component, or the `uninstall.sql` file when uninstalling our component.

Our next step will be to create these two files in our installation package. We will see the structure of our installer, updated with the SQL files, in a moment. But for now, just create the files.

Note that we have also added these two files to the administration part of our XML file. They will be placed inside the `admin` folder of our installer.

We will start with the `install.sql` file:

```
DROP TABLE IF EXISTS `#__tinynews`;

CREATE TABLE `#__tinynews` (
`id` INT NOT NULL AUTO_INCREMENT PRIMARY KEY,
`title` VARCHAR( 255 ) NOT NULL ,
`text` TEXT NOT NULL
) ;
```

The file contains two SQL sentences. The first one will drop the table if it already existed, so we can start with a new installation. The second one will actually create the table. Note that we are again using the #__ prefix, instead of placing the prefix ourselves.

Our `uninstall.sql` file will be even simpler:

```
DROP TABLE IF EXISTS `#__tinynews`;
```

But what if we don't want to drop the table during installation? This may be because we have created an updated version of our component. Then, instead of dropping the table and creating it later, we will have the following query in our `install.sql` file:

```
CREATE TABLE IF NOT EXISTS `#__tinynews` (
`id` INT NOT NULL AUTO_INCREMENT PRIMARY KEY,
`title` VARCHAR( 255 ) NOT NULL,
`text` TEXT NOT NULL
) ;
```

This will make sure the table is created if it does not already exist, but leave it alone if it does.

 You can find the updated code for our component in the `com_tinynews_step_3` folder of the code bundle.

Coding a basic admin zone

Well, we have made some good advances in building our component, but still much work needs to be done. One of these important steps, which still needs to be done, is the creation of an admin zone for our component.

With an admin zone, we will be able to insert, edit, and delete records, and also list them, with no knowledge of SQL.

So, let's get started with our admin zone. First we are going to create a folder inside the `administrator/components` folder of our Joomla! installation. This folder will be called `com_tinynews` (exactly as in the frontend part). In this folder, we will create two empty files: `index.html` and `tinynews.php`.

We can take a look to our component admin zone. If you remember, when working with our frontend, we were able to take a look at our component by using the following URL:

`http://www.yoursite.com/index.php?option=com_tinynews`.

Something similar can be done in our site administrator screen. Log in to your administration screen, and use the following URL:

`http://www.yoursite.com/administrator/index.php?option=com_tinynews`.

For now we will only be seeing an empty screen. But it won't take too much time for us to create a full admin panel here. First, we are going to fill our `administrator/components/com_tinynews/tinynews.php` file, as follows:

```php
<?php
defined( '_JEXEC' ) or die( 'Restricted access' );

require_once( JPATH_COMPONENT.DS.'controller.php' );

$controller   = new TinynewsController();

$controller->execute($task = null);
```

This file, as in our frontend part, will act as an entry point to our component, and will load the necessary controller. The controller that we are going to create just now will be created in `administrator/components/com_tinynews/controller.php` and will contain this code:

```php
<?php
defined( '_JEXEC' ) or die( 'Restricted access' );

jimport('joomla.application.component.controller');
```

```
class TinynewsController extends JController{

    function display(){
        parent::display();
    }

}
```

It's not much for now, but let's continue working. We will also need a model for our administrator screen. For now, we are going to just copy the one we had for our frontend. It will be in administrator/components/com_tinynews/models/tinynews.php and, if you remember, it was as follows:

```
<?php

defined( '_JEXEC' ) or die( 'Restricted access' );

jimport( 'joomla.application.component.model' );

class TinynewsModelTinynews extends JModel{
    function getallnews(){

        $database =& JFactory::getDBO();

        $query = "SELECT * FROM ".
                    $database->nameQuote('#__tinynews').";";

        $database->setQuery($query);
        $result = $database->loadObjectList();
        return $result;
    }
}
```

No modifications for now. Later we will come back to this file. Now let's work in our view.

Notice that the structure of the admin part is quite similar to the one we had for our frontend.

Our `views` folder will be placed in `administrator/components/com_tinynews`. Inside this folder, we will create another folder called `tinynews`, and inside that folder we will create a file called `view.html.php`. So, to summarize all these routes a bit, we will end up with the following path: `administrator/components/com_tinynews/views/tinynews/view.html.php`.

And what will be inside this `view.html.php` file? For now we will create it exactly as before, as follows:

```php
<?php
defined( '_JEXEC' ) or die( 'Restricted access' );

jimport( 'joomla.application.component.view');

class TinynewsViewTinynews extends JView{

    function display(){

        $model =& $this->getModel();

        $news = $model->getallnews();
        $this->assignRef('news', $news);

        parent::display();
    }
}
```

But we are going to introduce some modifications to this code in the display method to be more accurate. So our display method is going to look like this:

```php
function display(){

    JToolBarHelper::title('Tinynews', 'generic.png' );
    JToolBarHelper::deleteList();
    JToolBarHelper::editListX();
    JToolBarHelper::addNewX();

    $model =& $this->getModel();

    $news = $model->getallnews();
    $this->assignRef('news', $news);

    parent::display();
}
```

These `JToolBarHelper` commands will be in charge of creating the buttons for our admin screen and the rest of the code will, as before, take all the data from our table and present it to us on our screen.

But for that to happen, we will need one more file, just one more I promise you!

This file will be a template file called `default.php` and will be placed in `administrator/components/com_tinynews/views/tinynews/tmpl`.

This file will be a bit different to the one we had for our frontend. Take a look at its content:

```php
<?php defined('_JEXEC') or die('Restricted access'); ?>

<form action="index.php" method="post" name="adminForm">
<div id="editcell">
    <table class="adminlist">
    <thead>
        <tr>
            <th width="5">
                Id
            </th>
            <th>
                Title
            </th>
            <th>
                Text
            </th>
        </tr>
    </thead>
    <?php

    $i = 0;
    foreach($this->news as $new){

    ?>
        <tr class="<?php echo "row$i"; ?>">
            <td>
                <?php echo $new->id; ?>
            </td>
            <td>
                <?php echo $new->title; ?>
            </td>
            <td>
                <?php echo $new->text; ?>
```

```
                    </td>
              </tr>
              <?php

              $i = 1 - $i;
          }
          ?>
          </table>
    </div>

    <input type="hidden" name="option" value="com_tinynews" />
    <input type="hidden" name="task" value="" />
    <input type="hidden" name="boxchecked" value="0" />

    </form>
```

Don't try to copy all this code, as it will be in the code bundle. Keep with us while we comment on this code.

As you have seen, first we create a form. This will be of use later, when we need to post which actions are being selected by users, (which records, among others).

The CSS classes and the ids are from the Joomla! admin template. So we don't need to define them, and our component will look similar to the other ones, which is exactly what we want.

Then we loop through our records — the ones that were retrieved thanks to our model. We also did that in the frontend, so there are not many changes here. Except, maybe, for the following code:

```
class="<?php echo "row$i"; ?>"
```

It takes care of creating `tr` with class `row0` or `row1`, depending on the contents of the `$i` variable.

Towards the end we can see some hidden fields. The first one tells the option, `com_tinynews`, the second the task, and the last one is called `boxchecked`. We will talk about the last field later.

The two first will tell Joomla! the component and the task, be it add, edit, or delete.

Why don't we take a look at the result of our efforts? If you go to `http://www.yoursite.com/administrator/index.php?option=com_tinynews`, you will see a screen that looks more or less like the next screenshot:

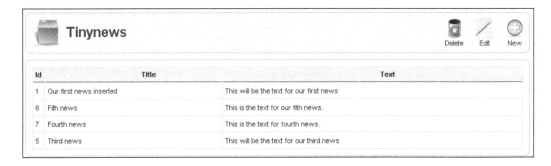

Id	Title	Text
1	Our first news inserted	This will be the text for our first news
8	Fith news	This is the text for our fith news.
7	Fourth news	This is the text for fourth news.
5	Third news	This will be the text for our third news

Ah, the look and feel of a typical Joomla! component. There's still some work to be done, but first things first. This is a great time to update our XML file, so let's do that as follows:

```
<administration>

<menu>Component Tinynews</menu>

<files folder="admin">
  ...
  <filename>controller.php</filename>
  <filename>models/index.html</filename>
  <filename>models/tinynews.php</filename>
  <filename>views/index.html</filename>
  <filename>views/tinynews/index.html</filename>
  <filename>views/tinynews/view.hmtl.php</filename>
  <filename>views/tinynews/tmpl/index.html</filename>
  <filename>views/tinynews/tmpl/default.php</filename>
</files>

</administration>
```

As you can see, we have only modified the administration part. Don't forget that all these files also need to be included in our installer file.

> This new step in the development of our component can be found in `com_tinynews_step_4` folder for the code bundle of Chapter 8. If you are lost, maybe you want to take a look there.

Of all these files, the ones inside the `admin` folder will go into `administrator/components/com_tinynews` and the ones inside the `site` folder will go into `components/com_tinynews`.

We have done very good work till now, but there are many things still left to do in our component. Hey, these are the more interesting ones, so stay with us!

Inserting, editing, and deleting records in our admin zone

All these actions are very basic for any admin zone, and we are going to create them in our own. For users to be able to perform these actions we placed some buttons that we did in our view, `administrator/components/com_tinynews/views/tinynews/view.html.php`, as follows:

```
function display(){

    JToolBarHelper::title('Tinynews', 'generic.png' );
    JToolBarHelper::deleteList();
    JToolBarHelper::editListX();
    JToolBarHelper::addNewX();

    $model =& $this->getModel();

    $news = $model->getallnews();
    $this->assignRef('news', $news);

    parent::display();
}
```

The new button doesn't need more information, but the delete and edit ones will need something more: the records they will take action to. For this we will pass the ID of the records, and to do this we are going to add some checkboxes to the listing screen.

We will do that in template file, `administrator/components/com_tinynews/views/tinynews/tmpl/default.php`, as follows:

```
<?php defined('_JEXEC') or die('Restricted access'); ?>

<form action="index.php" method="post" name="adminForm">
<div id="editcell">
    <table class="adminlist">
    <thead>
```

```
            <tr>
                <th width="5">
                 <input type="checkbox" name="toggle" value=""
                 onclick="checkAll(<?php echo count( $this->news ); ?>);"
                  />
                </th>
                <th width="5">
                    Id
                </th>
                <th>
                    Title
                </th>
                <th>
                    Text
                </th>
            </tr>
        </thead>
        <?php

    $i = 0;
    $row = 0;
    foreach($this->news as $new){

    ?>
        <tr class="<?php echo "row$i"; ?>">
            <td>
              <?php echo JHTML::_( 'grid.id', $row, $new->id ); ?>
            </td>
            <td>
                <?php echo $new->id; ?>
            </td>
            <td>
                <a href="<?php echo JRoute::_(
                'index.php?option=com_tinynews&task=edit&cid[]='
                $new->id ); ?>"><?php echo $new->title; ?></a>
            </td>
            <td>
                <?php echo $new->text; ?>
            </td>
        </tr>
        <?php
        $row++;
        $i = 1 - $i;
    }
    ?>
```

```
      </table>
  </div>

  <input type="hidden" name="option" value="com_tinynews" />
  <input type="hidden" name="task" value="" />
  <input type="hidden" name="boxchecked" value="0" />

  </form>
```

I've placed in bold the changes, so we can concentrate on them. Take for example the first change:

```
<input type="checkbox" name="toggle" value=""
  onclick="checkAll(<?php echo count( $this->news ); ?>);" />
```

With this code we are creating a checkbox that, when clicked, will select all the other checkboxes that we have. For this we are going to use the checkAll JavaScript method that comes with Joomla!.

The parameter we pass to the checkAll method will be the number of expected checkboxes. We will do that by counting the news variable. With this we will help to select or deselect all the checkboxes with only one click.

Next we are adding the $row variable:

```
  $row = 0;
```

This will help us to count the number of rows. While we are in the loop, this will be of use for our next addition:

```
<td>
  <?php echo JHTML::_( 'grid.id', $row, $new->id ); ?>
</td>
```

This requires a bit of explanation. But in short, it creates a checkbox using the $row value to name each checkbox and distinguish each one from the others. The $new->id value will be used to give these checkboxes their value.

So at the end, we will have one checkbox for row and this checkbox will contain the ID value for the record so that when deleting or editing we know which record we are working with.

Now for the long explanation: we are using the JHTML utility class, which will in turn call the grid class and its method id. The other two parameters work as we have commented before.

If you want to know more about these classes, you can take a look at the following URLs:

- `http://api.joomla.org/Joomla-Framework/HTML/JHTML.html`
- `http://api.joomla.org/Joomla-Framework/HTML/JHTMLGrid.html`

Our next step will be to transform the title field, from a simple text to a link, as follows:

```
<a href="<?php echo JRoute::_( 'index.php?option=com_tinynews&task=
edit&cid[]='. $new->id ); ?>"><?php echo $new->title; ?></a>
```

This way we won't need to select the checkbox, and after that, click on the edit button. With this link we will do the same with only one click. Here we use `JRoute` to create our link, but note that we are also sending some variables, as follows, with this URL:

- `option` — will be our component, `com_tinynews`
- `task` — will be `edit` in this case
- `id` of the element — it will be `$new->id`

At the end of all this work, we will end up with something like the next screenshot:

Nice, but aren't we missing something? Yes, all the things necessary to add, edit, or delete new records. Why don't we work on that now?

First, we are going to modify our entry point that's the `administrator/components/com_tinynews/tinynews.php` file a bit. We are going to change the `$controller->execute($task = null);` line to this:

```
$controller->execute( JRequest::getVar( 'task', 'null' ) );

$controller->redirect();
```

We are taking the `task` variable that was sent from our form so that we can call the `controller` method that is required. Also, we are adding the `redirect` method just in case a controller has set a redirect, as will be the case with some of them.

With these changes our entry point is ready. Our next file is going to be the controller, as much work needs to be done there. Just open the `administrator/components/com_tinynews/controller.php` file.

If you remember, in our view file we had something like this:

```
JToolBarHelper::deleteList();
JToolBarHelper::editListX();
JToolBarHelper::addNewX();
```

These calls to the `JToolBarHelper` methods were used to create the buttons of our admin zone, and when clicked, these will be used to send the task we want to do. Our entry point file will then execute the controller method, whose task is equal to the task sent by the button.

But it seems no task is being passed to these methods. Well, in fact, they will send a default task, for example:

- `JToolBarHelper::deleteList()` → `$task = 'remove'`
- `JToolBarHelper::editListX()` → `$task = 'edit'`
- `JToolBarHelper::addNewX` → `$task = 'add'`

There's much more to learn about the `JtoolBarHelper`, and to do so you can take a look to these links:

`http://docs.joomla.org/JToolBarHelper`

`http://docs.joomla.org/JToolBarHelper/custom`

Other tasks can be sent instead of the default ones, but we are going to use those, so the only thing we need to do is to add methods with those names to our controller. Let's do that, as follows:

```
function __construct(){
    parent::__construct();
    $this->registerTask( 'add'  ,       'edit' );
}
```

First we are adding a constructor method just so we can use the `registerTask` method in it. What does this method do? It just redirects and remaps all calls to the method passed as a first parameter to the method passed as second parameter.

So all calls to the `add` method will be redirected to the `edit` one, saving us of having to create two methods, where using one will be enough. Now let us take a look at the edit method:

```
function edit(){
    JRequest::setVar( 'view', 'addnews' );
    JRequest::setVar( 'layout', 'form'  );
    JRequest::setVar('hidemainmenu', 1);

    parent::display();
}
```

Here we are defining three things:

- The view file to use
- The layout of that view to use
- We are hiding the main menu of the admin zone; in fact, more than hiding, we are disabling it

We are done with our edit method, and next will be the `remove` method, as follows:

```
function remove(){
    $model = $this->getModel('addnews');

    if(!$model->delete()) {
        $msg = "One or more records couldn't be deleted";
    } else {
        $msg = "Records deleted ok";
    }

    $this->setRedirect( 'index.php?option=com_tinynews', $msg );
}
```

This method is also quite easy. First we load our `model`, which we will be created later, and then we try to call the `delete` method of our model, creating a message variable that will contain one message or another, depending on whether our `delete` method is able to delete the record or not.

Lastly, we set a redirect so that after all the deleting process has finished our page will be redirected. Remember that in our entry point file we have `$controller->redirect();`.

So the redirect method will, in fact, execute the previously set redirect. Note that in the `setRedirect` method we have a second parameter, which will contain the message that will be shown after the page is redirected.

With this we have prepared all methods necessary for add, edit, and remove. Well, not all of the add and edit methods, though they are only ones and are used to just load the views and templates necessary. But they are not calling any model method: I mean, no data is being saved to the database.

In order to really save data, we are going to create another method in our controller. We are going to name it `save`.

```
function save(){
    $model = $this->getModel('addnews');

    if ($model->savedata()) {
        $msg = "News saved.";
    } else {
        $msg = "News couldn't be saved.";
    }

    $this->setRedirect( 'index.php?option=com_tinynews', $msg);
}
```

It is not much different from our `remove` method. We load our model, call one of its methods to do our task, and then we set a redirect to return to the main page of our admin panel.

The method we are going to call is the `savedata` one. Don't worry, we will be working on that soon. But first, there's still one more method we need to create, the `cancel` one:

```
function cancel(){
    $msg = "Action cancelled";
    $this->setRedirect( 'index.php?option=com_tinynews', $msg );
}
```

There's much here, but it's very necessary indeed, as it will be used to return to our admin main screen when we want to cancel an action.

Now that we have built a good base here, we are almost done! I know you are waiting to see the model, but we will be working on the view file first.

So we are going to create a new view file in our `edit` controller method we had:

```
JRequest::setVar( 'view', 'addnews' );
```

We were setting that we wanted to use our `addnews` view. This view doesn't exist at the moment, so we are going to create it. We will also need to create a new folder. In the end, we will have this path: `administrator/components/com_tinynews/views/addnews/view.html.php`. In this file, we will have:

```php
<?php
defined( '_JEXEC' ) or die( 'Restricted access' );

jimport( 'joomla.application.component.view');

class TinynewsViewAddnews extends JView{

    function display(){

        $news = $this->get('Data');
        $exists = ($news->id < 1);

        $text = $exists ? "New" : "Edit";

        JToolBarHelper::title(   "News".': <small>[ ' . $text.' ]
        </small>' );
        JToolBarHelper::save();

        if ($exists)  {
            JToolBarHelper::cancel();
        } else {
            JToolBarHelper::cancel( 'cancel', 'Close' );
        }

        $this->assignRef('news', $news);
        parent::display();
    }

}
```

I know it's a bit hard to understand all what is happening without having seen the model, but try to get the basics of what is happening here. Later, when we have been through all the files, you will be able to read it again, and most importantly, try it yourself in your own Joomla! installation.

Now back to our view file. As we can see, we have the following naming convention:

```
TinynewsViewAddnews
```

It is, as we have commented before, denoted as `Componentname`**`View`**`Viewname`. Also note that our view automatically has access to the model with the same name as the view name. So we call one of our model methods to get the data:

```
$news = $this->get('Data');
```

With this data, we can check if the id is lower than 1:

```
$exists = ($news->id < 1);
```

If the ID was to be lower than one, it would mean that it doesn't exist, so we should be working with a new record instead of editing an existing one. This will help us to determine if we are creating a new record or editing it, and place the corresponding texts on our toolbar title.

With the toolbar methods, we define the `title` and the `save` button:

```
JToolBarHelper::title( "News".': <small>[ ' . $text.' ]</small>' );
    JToolBarHelper::save();
```

Next we check if the record exists or if it is a new one. If it's a new one, we will have a cancel button. However, if it already exists, we will have the same button, but it will have the text `Close` in it:

```
if ($exists)  {
    JToolBarHelper::cancel();
} else {
    JToolBarHelper::cancel( 'cancel', 'Close' );
}
```

Next we only need to assign a new variable, so we will have the data available in our template file:

```
$this->assignRef('news', $news);
```

This template file will be extremely easy to follow. Ready to create it? We will create it in `administrator/components/com_tinynews/views/addnews/tmpl/form.php`, as follows:

```php
<?php defined('_JEXEC') or die('Restricted access'); ?>

<form action="index.php" method="post" name="adminForm"
id="adminForm">
<div class="col100">
    <fieldset class="adminform">
        <legend>News' details</legend>
        <table class="admintable">
        <tr>
            <td width="100" align="right" class="key">
                <label for="title">
                    Title:
                </label>
            </td>
            <td>
              <input class="text_area" type="text" name="title"
              id="title" value="<?php echo $this->news->title;?>"
              size="40"/>
            </td>
        </tr>
        <tr>
            <td width="100" align="right" class="key">
                <label for="title">
                    Text:
                </label>
            </td>
            <td>
              <textarea class="text_area" type="text" name="text"
              id="text" cols="40" rows="5"><?php echo $this->
              news->text;?></textarea>
            </td>
        </tr>
    </table>
    </fieldset>
</div>

<div class="clr"></div>

<input type="hidden" name="option" value="com_tinynews" />
<input type="hidden" name="id" value="<?php echo $this->news->id; ?>"
/>
<input type="hidden" name="task" value="" />
</form>
```

This form is mostly as any form you could have seen everywhere; the only thing to note here is the way we set the value of the inputs:

```
value="<?php echo $this->news->title;?>"
```

As you can see, we are using the **news** variable we have set in the view before. Of course, this will only work when editing.

Now I want you to see something that we haven't said a word about: a `table` class. A `table` class will greatly help us in working with the database.

At the moment our table is quite small. But imagine if we were working with a table with ten columns. It would be quite tedious to write, insert, or update queries. Our table class will greatly help us with that.

First create the `addnews.php` file. It will be in the `administrator/components/com_tinynews/tables` folder and will be as follows:

```php
<?php
defined( '_JEXEC' ) or die( 'Restricted access' );

class TableAddnews extends JTable{

  var $id = null;
  var $title = null;
  var $text = null;

  function TableAddnews(& $db) {
    parent::__construct('#__tinynews', 'id', $db);
  }

}
```

Soon you will be surprised that something so small could help us so much. In fact, we are only defining some properties for the class, one property for each database field. Then, we override the database constructor. This is necessary so that we can define the table we are working with. This would be the first parameter, the next one will define the field that is our Primary Key, and the last one is an instance of the database connector.

That's all! Next stop, our model file. We have waited long enough for this. Let's take a look into it. It well help us understand what has been happening with all that data coming and going.

The model file, `addnews.php`, will be placed in `administrator/components/com_tinynews/models`, and will be as follows:

```php
<?php

defined( '_JEXEC' ) or die( 'Restricted access' );

jimport( 'joomla.application.component.model' );

class TinynewsModelAddnews extends JModel{

    function &getData(){

        // Get data code will be here
    }

    function savedata(){

        // Save data code will be here
    }

    function delete(){

      // Delete code will be here

    }

}
```

We have three methods in our model, each one with a different task. We are going to see them one by one. Let's start with the first one:

```php
function &getData(){

    $array = JRequest::getVar('cid',  0, '', 'array');
    $id = $array[0];

    $query = ' SELECT * FROM #__tinynews WHERE id = '.$id;
    $this->_db->setQuery( $query );
    $data = $this->_db->loadObject();

    if (!$data) {
        $data = new stdClass();
```

```
        $data->id = 0;
        $data->title = null;
        $data->text = null;
    }
    return $data;
}
```

I want to note something here. If we recap a bit, in our view, we had this code:

```
$news = $this->get('Data');
```

That piece of code called our getData method of our model. How is that? Well, methods that start with get in our model can be called with get() in our view. So $this->get('Data'); is in fact calling the getData() method.

Most of the code here is quite easy to follow. First we try to get the cid variable, which we defined in our link or when clicking on the **Edit** button of our admin zone. We then try to get the first element, just in case more than one record has been selected, as we can only edit one element at a time.

Next, we query the database and use the loadObject method in order to retrieve the record, but if no record is returned we create an empty one so that no error is shown in the edit screen when trying to get the properties of the object. Then we return the data. That's all!

The savedata method is not going to be much harder either, and is as follows:

```
function savedata(){

    $row =& $this->getTable('addnews');

    if (!$row->bind( JRequest::get( 'post' ) )) {
        $this->setError($this->_db->getErrorMsg());
        return false;
    }

    if (!$row->check()) {
        $this->setError($this->_db->getErrorMsg());
        return false;
    }

    if (!$row->store()) {
        $this->setError($this->_db->getErrorMsg());
```

```
            return false;
        }
        return true;
    }
```

First of all we get our table class. Here we are going to see how we can use it:

```
$row->bind( JRequest::get( 'post' ) )
```

The bind method will fill every property of the table class with the values sent by the form.

 Note that our form input fields were named exactly as the table class properties, which also equals table field names. This is something important.

The `bind` method will prepare the data to be inserted or updated. See how easy it is? It is much easier than writing an insert query or an update one. But before trying to insert the data, we check whether it's okay with `$row->check()`. This checks if we have all the fields we expect so that we can process to the store method `$row->store()`.

`$row->store()` will be the one in charge of saving the data, whether it be by inserting it, or updating an existing record. This is a small table, but for larger ones the difference between using a table class or not will be greatly noticeable. I highly advise using table classes.

Now only one left—the `delete` method. It is as follows:

```
function delete(){
    $cids = JRequest::getVar( 'cid', array(0), 'post', 'array' );

    $row =& $this->getTable('addnews');

    foreach($cids as $cid) {
        if (!$row->delete( $cid )) {
            $this->setError( $row->getErrorMsg() );
            return false;
        }
    }
    return true;
}
```

As before, we get the IDs of the records to delete, load the table class, and one ID after another we delete by using `$row->delete( $cid )`.

And that's all! We are done! Our component is able to delete, edit, or add new records to the database. Mostly, our component will look similar to the following screenshot:

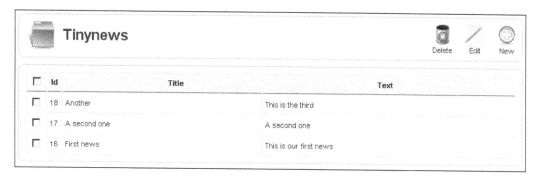

But also in the next screenshot, we can see a "new" element form:

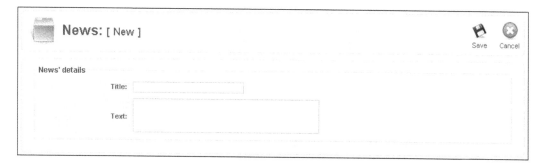

But better than seeing this on some images, why don't you try it by yourself? You only need to go to `http://www.yoursite.com/administrator/index.php?option=com_tinynews`.

Also remember that we must reflect these changes in our package installer XML file:

```
<files folder="admin">
<filename>tinynews.php</filename>
<filename>index.html</filename>
<filename>install.sql</filename>
<filename>uninstall.sql</filename>
<filename>controller.php</filename>
<filename>models/index.html</filename>
<filename>models/tinynews.php</filename>
```

```
<filename>models/addnews.php</filename>
<filename>views/index.html</filename>
<filename>views/tinynews/index.html</filename>
<filename>views/tinynews/view.hmtl.php</filename>
<filename>views/tinynews/tmpl/index.html</filename>
<filename>views/tinynews/tmpl/default.php</filename>
<filename>views/addnews/index.html</filename>
<filename>views/addnews/view.hmtl.php</filename>
<filename>views/addnews/tmpl/index.html</filename>
<filename>views/addnews/tmpl/form.php</filename>
<filename>tables/addnews.php</filename>
<filename>tables/index.html</filename>
</files>
```

You can find this final stage in the `com_tinynews_step_5` folder of our component in the code bundle of the book in Chapter 8. There you will find all the code we have been working with.

Note that before this point, our installer package won't be fully functional, resulting in errors or problems. Now it's fully safe for us to install our extension with our installation package.

At this point, we are able to install our extension from the Administrator screen of our Joomla! installation, just as any other extension from the **Extensions | Install/Uninstall** menu.

After installing our extension, it will appear under the **Components** menu the way we see in the next screenshot:

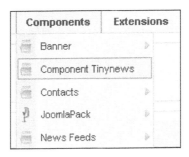

With this link, we will be able to go to our components main page. Also, if we go to **Menus | Main Menu** and click on the **New** button, we will be able to see that our component can also be linked on any Joomla! menu:

This way we are able to create a new entry in our main site menu, just like the one shown in the following screenshot:

As we can see, our component behaves much like any other Joomla! component. We have done good work here.

Now maybe you want to give it a try yourself; this way you will better understand how everything works.

Showing our data in our module

Now that we have inserted some data into the database, it's the best time to modify our module and enhance it to show this data in our module position.

At the moment, `mod_tinynews` is only showing the "This is working" message, which obviously is useful for nothing. Let's enhance it. The first file that we are going to modify is `modules/mod_tinynews/helper.php`, as follows:

```php
<?php
defined('_JEXEC') or die('Direct Access to this location is not
allowed.');

class ModTinyNewsHelper{
```

```
function getallnews(){

    $database =& JFactory::getDBO();

    $query = "SELECT * FROM ".$database->nameQuote('#__
      tinynews').";";

    $database->setQuery($query);

    $result = $database->loadObjectList();

    return $result;
    }
}
```

Looks familiar? It's the same method we used in our component frontend model. It will be useful for here too. We will call this method in our modules/mod_tinynews/mod_tinynews.php file:

```
<?php
defined('_JEXEC') or die('Direct Access to this location is not
allowed.');

JHTML::stylesheet('styles.css','modules/mod_tinynews/css/');

$document =& JFactory::getDocument();
$document->addscript(JURI::root(true).'modules'.DS.'mod_tinynews'.
DS.'js'.DS.'tinynews.js');

require_once(dirname(__FILE__).DS.'helper.php');

$news = ModTinynewsHelper::getallnews();

require(JModuleHelper::getLayoutPath('mod_tinynews','default_tmpl'));
```

The only difference here is that we are calling the `getallnews` method from our helper. This way we will have the result in our `$news` variable that will be available in our modules/mod_tinynews/default_tmpl.php file:

```
<?php
defined('_JEXEC') or die('Direct Access to this location is not
allowed.');
?>
<div id="tinynews">

<?php
  foreach($news as $new){
```

```
    echo "<p><b>".$new->title."</b></p><br/><br/>";
    echo "<p>".$new->text."</p><br/><br/>";

    }
?>

</div>
```

This code is also quite similar to the one we used in our component, but instead of using $this->news for getting the value from a class property, we now have our variable directly available as $news. With all this code in place, our module will look similar to the following screenshot:

First news

Text for the first news

Second one

This is the text for the second news

Third one

This is the third text

Better than before, isn't it? But we will make it even better soon.

> You can find the modified module in the second_mod_tinynews.tar.gz file in the code bundle, so you can take a look at it.

Adding jQuery to our module—refreshing data using JavaScript

Making our module look better is quite easy, as we are only using plain HTML for now. A bit of jQuery won't do any harm; in fact, it will look much better.

For this example, I've one jQuery plugin in mind: the Vertical news ticker plugin. We can find it on the jQuery site by searching for "Vertical news ticker", or we can download it at the following link:

`http://plugins.jquery.com/project/vTicker`.

Download the plugin, place the `jquery.vticker.js` file in `modules/mod_tinynews/js/`, and we are done. We have the necessary tool for our example. Our next step will be to change the `modules/mod_tinynews/tmpl/default_tmpl.php` file, just some cosmetic changes, as follows:

```php
<?php
defined('_JEXEC') or die('Direct Access to this location is not
allowed.');
?>
<div id="tinynews">
  <ul>

<?php
  foreach($news as $new){

    echo "<li>";
    echo "<b>".$new->title."</b><br/><br/>";
    echo "".nl2br($new->text)."<br/><br/>";
    echo "</li>";

  }
?>
  </ul>
</div>
```

We have prepared an unordered list of elements; the plugin will need that to move the elements. Our next change is in the `modules/mod_tinynews/mod_tinynews.php` file. Here we need to add the highlighted code:

```
. . .
$document =& JFactory::getDocument();
$document->addscript(JURI::root(true).'modules'.DS.'mod_tinynews'
          .DS.'js'.DS.'jquery.vticker.js');
$document->addscript(JURI::root(true).'modules'.DS.'mod_tinynews'
          .DS.'js'.DS.'tinynews.js');
. . .
```

This will load the necessary jQuery plugin. Now we need to make the necessary plugin call. We will be doing that in our `modules/mod_tinynews/js/tinynews.js` file. We will replace its current contents with the following code:

```
jQuery(document).ready(function($){
   $('#tinynews').vTicker({
      speed: 2000,
      pause: 4000,
      showItems: 1,
      animation: 'fade',
      mousePause: true
   });

});
```

We are calling the `vTicker` function on the `#tinynews` DIV — that's the DIV containing our unordered list of news. Let's take a quick look at the options:

- `speed` — here we can define the speed of the scroll animation
- `pause` — is the time between each scrolling action
- `showItems` — is used for stating the number of items to be visible
- `animation` — here we can use fade, for a fade in or out animation, or leave the default for a sliding animation
- `mousePause` — having this set to `true` will stop the animation when the mouse pointer is over the ticker

These options will be very useful to modify the resulting effect. For example, I've added some more texts to our news, and our module now looks similar to the following screenshot:

at congue elit feugiat eu. In tortor lorem, faucibus sed feugiat vel, hendrerit ut leo. Donec mi ligula, adipiscing ac vestibulum eget, sagittis quis nisi. Nunc at velit ut nisi vulputate dictum at vitae augue.

Third one

This is the third text.

Lorem ipsum dolor sit amet, consectetur adipiscing elit. Nunc sollicitudin lectus ut dolor hendrerit consequat. Sed dictum ultrices sapien,

I've tried to capture the moment of the fade, but it's much better to see it in action, so why don't you give it a try?

Summary

Well, this chapter has come to an end. I really hope you liked it, and it has been useful for you. With this chapter we have taken a big step forward. Now we are able to build our own components and make them work along with other components.

This way we are able to build stronger solutions with more complex and a lot more development options. We have also added a bit of jQuery to our module. But don't worry, in the next chapter we will be adding much more.

Now take some rest and get prepared. The next chapter is going to be even better. Don't forget to try all the things you have learned in this chapter, as they will help you better understand what we have been doing.

9

Going Further with Our Component Development

"Always take care of the details; the difference lies there."

At the end of our last chapter, we made a working component and a little module that, though it was quite simple, enabled us to show our news to visitors. We saw the basics of working with data (such as inserting data, editing, and eventually deleting it) in a Joomla! component.

In this chapter, we will keep working with that component, but try and make it even better, more useful, and with a better interface. I'm sure that at this point in time, all of us want to make some more interesting jQuery features, and that's what we are trying to do in this chapter.

We will be working on both the admin screen and the frontend of our component. Both parts are quite important, and we need to take care of them. In this chapter, we will look at the following topics:

- Adding a table paginator plugin to our admin zone
- The textarea autogrow plugin
- Working a bit on our component's frontpage
  - ° Creating equal size columns with jQuery
  - ° Paginating our contents
- Going back to the admin zone
  - ° Adding tips and instructions to fill our form using JavaScript
  - ° Uploading images

- Showing our images on the frontend
  - ○ An interesting way to show a caption
  - ○ A different "full size" image

- Adding a WYSIWYG editor to our component's backend

At the end of this chapter, not only will we have a working component, but also one that looks pretty good. Don't wait any longer, let's start.

Adding a table paginator plugin to our admin zone

First, we will add an interesting plugin to our component administrator screen, for example, a table paginator plugin. We are going to use the plugin we can find here:

`http://slashjquery.com/`.

The plugin is called tablePager (made by Rasmus Styrk), and it will help divide any table we want into pages. Of course, we can do that with the help of Joomla!'s functions. But hey, after all we are in a Joomla! and jQuery book, so using a jQuery plugin will be fine.

> If you are interested in learning more about Joomla! pagination, you can take a look at the following link:
>
> `http://docs.joomla.org/Using_JPagination_in_your_component`.
>
> It's a very interesting article.

First, download the plugin and place the `jquery.tablePager-1.2.js` file in `administrator/components/com_tinynews/js/`. Later we will see how to use it. Now we will proceed to our administrator screen, `components/com_tinynews`. On that screen, if you have inserted some news, you will see a screen just like the following screenshot:

If you don't have enough news records, try to insert some, as we are going to need them. We will now work with one of the template files. Open the `administrator/ components/com_tinynews/views/tinynews/tmpl/default.php` file. At the beginning we have:

```php
<?php defined('_JEXEC') or die('Restricted access'); ?>

<form action="index.php" method="post" name="adminForm">
```

Add the highlighted code into this section:

```php
<?php

defined('_JEXEC') or die('Restricted access');

$js = JURI::base().'components/com_tinynews/js/
    jquery.tablePager-1.2.js';
$document =& JFactory::getDocument();
$document->addScript($js);
```

As you can see in the highlighted code, we are first creating the path to the jQuery plugin. For this we use the JURI base method and add the path to the folder where we have placed the plugin.

After that we take an instance of the document and use the `addScript` method in order to add the script to the header of our document. After doing that, if we refresh our document admin page and take a look at the source code for the page, we will be able to see the following code:

```
<script type="text/javascript"
        src="http://wayofthewebninja.com/administrator/
             components/com_tinynews/js/
             jquery.tablePager-1.2.js"></script>
```

With this in place, we are now able to use the plugin functions. The basic usage for the plugin would look mostly like this:

```
$js = "
  jQuery(document).ready(function($){
    $('.adminlist').tablePager();
  });
";
$document->addScriptDeclaration($js);
```

We will add this code just below the previous `script` tag just to ensure that it will be executed after the plugin has been included. This code is quite simple; we call the `tablePager` method upon the elements with `adminlist` class. The result of this code will be our table divided into pages. By default, the plugin will create a page for each of the five elements, and without styling, our table will look like this:

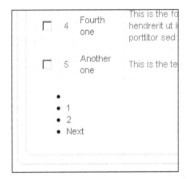

We are going to style this a bit, but just a bit will do. Create the stylesheet file, `styles.css`, and place it in `administrator/components/com_tinynews/css/`. Adding this stylesheet is quite similar to adding our `js` files. We will continue to work on our `default.php` file and add the stylesheet as follows:

```
  });

";
```

```
$document->addScriptDeclaration($js);

$css = JURI::base().'components/com_tinynews/css/styles.css';
$document->addStyleSheet( $css );
```

The `addStyleSheet` method works quite similarly to the `addScript` method, but for stylesheets instead of script files. With that code in place, our stylesheet will be loaded. So let's add some styles there:

```
.pagerLinks{
  width: 100%;
  margin-top: 20px;
}

.pagerLinks ul{
  text-align: center;
  margin: 0;
  padding: 0;
}

.pagerLinks ul li{
  list-style: none;
  display: inline;
  font-weight: bold;
  margin: 5px;
}

.pagerLinks li a:link, .pagerLinks li a:visited{
  color: #ffffff;
  background-color: #0087C5;
  padding: 5px 10px 5px 10px;
}

.pagerLinks li a:hover{
  color: #ffffff;
  background-color: #34393B;
  padding: 5px 10px 5px 10px;
}

.pagerLinks li a.active {
  color: #ffffff;
  background-color: #34393B;
  padding: 5px 10px 5px 10px;
}
```

The `pagerLinks` class is the container class for our paginator links. The plugin will create a DIV with this class and place the page links inside. The rest of styles are just for centering the links, giving them an interesting look. This can be seen in the following screenshot:

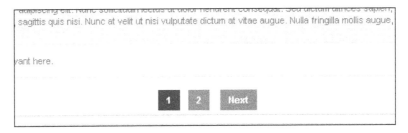

It's better now, isn't it? Of course, clicking on the links will result in the next page being loaded. We have placed some styles for the `pagerLinks` class elements. Though it was not so necessary in our example, we could have also styled some other classes like the following two, as it took the styling from the `pagerLinks` elements:

- `nextPage`
- `previousPage`

We can continue and add specific styles to these classes, but I think we should go on, so let's take a look at the other options of the plugin:

- `offset` — will be our starting page; the default is 0.
- `limit` — is the number of rows that will go into each page; the default is 5.
- `placeTop` — is false by default, and indicates if we want the `paginator` DIV to go on top or under the table; the default is under the table.

Let's see an example with all the options in place:

```
jQuery(document).ready(function($){
$('.adminlist').tablePager({ offset: 4, limit: 3, placeTop: true });
});
```

As you can see, here we are setting the starting row to be the fourth one, limiting each page to three rows, and placing the pagination on top of the table. In fact, it is quite easy to modify it.

We are finished with this first example. If you would like to give it a try, you can find the modifications to our component in the code bundle—except for the table paginator plugin, which you must download from here:

`http://slashjquery.com/.`

You can find the other two modified files in the `table_plugin` folder of the code bundle. Why don't you give it a try? After that you can continue with our next example.

Textarea autogrow plugin

For our next example, we are going to see a textarea autogrow plugin. This is going to be an easy one to use, but very useful in the insert and edit forms of our component. This time we are going to use the plugin from Antti Kaihola and we can find it here:

`http://github.com/akaihola/jquery-simpleautogrow.`

Download the packed file. Inside we will find a file called `jquery.simpleautogrow.js`. Place this file in the `administrator/components/com_tinynews/js` folder. After placing the file, we need to modify our `form.php` template file placed at `administrator/components/com_tinynews/views/addnews/tmpl/`. Remember how we declared our previous script? We are going to do something similar now:

```php
<?php

defined('_JEXEC') or die('Restricted access');

$js = JURI::base().'components/com_tinynews/js/jquery.simpleautogrow.js';
$document =& JFactory::getDocument();
$document->addScript($js);
```

The only difference is the name of the script we are loading. After that, we will make use of the plugin:

```php
$js = "
  jQuery(document).ready(function($){
    $('textarea').simpleautogrow();
  });
";
$document->addScriptDeclaration($js);
?>
```

As you can see, `simpleautogrow` is the function to call. With this simple call, our `textarea` will adapt its height to the amount of text it has. For example, in a fresh form, we would have something similar to the following screenshot:

If we try to write something in the `textarea`, we will see how it adapts to our text, as seen in the next screenshot:

```
        If we start writing.

        And then we need

        more and more

Text:   lines

        the textarea height

        will grow accordingly

        .|
```

Interesting, isn't it? This will help us provide a textarea that will automatically adapt to our needs, and incorporating it was very easy, thanks to the plugin. Our next stop is going to be the frontpage of our component.

But remember that you can find the modified `form.php` file in the `textarea_plugin` folder of Chapter 9 in the code bundle.

Working on our component's frontpage

Now that we have worked a bit on our admin zone, it's time for us to work on the frontpage of our component, just to make it look better. At the moment, our component only shows a list of news. If you take a look at the `components/com_tinynews/views/tinynews/tmpl/default.php` file, you will see our previous code:

```
defined('_JEXEC') or die('Restricted access');

foreach($this->news as $new){
```

```
echo "<p><b>".$new->title."</b></p><br/><br/>";
echo "<p>".$new->text."</p><br/><br/>";
}
```

We are going to change this code a bit, as follows:

```
defined('_JEXEC') or die('Restricted access');

foreach($this->news as $new){
?>
  <div class="news_box">
    <h1><?php echo $new->title; ?></h1>
    <p><?php echo $new->text; ?></p>
  </div>
<?php
}
```

These are only small changes, but they are necessary if we want to add some styling later. For this, we are going to create a CSS file. We will create this file (called frontend_style.css) inside components/com_tinynews/css/, and we will place some styles in it, as follows:

```
.news_box{
  width: 175px;
  margin-right: 9px;
  margin-bottom: 9px;
  float: left;
  border-right: 1px solid #3B3630;
  border-bottom: 1px solid #3B3630;
}

.news_box h1{
  font-size: 16px;
  font-weight: bold;
  margin-bottom: 10px;
  padding-right: 10px;
}

.news_box p{
  padding-right: 10px;
}
```

After we have our basic styles in place, we need to include the CSS file. We will do that in our `components/com_tinynews/views/tinynews/tmpl/default.php` file:

```
defined('_JEXEC') or die('Restricted access');

$document =& JFactory::getDocument();
$css = JURI::base().'components/com_tinynews/css/frontend_style.css';
$document->addStyleSheet( $css );
```

Just as we have seen on our admin screen, we will use the `addStyleSheet` method, and with that done, our component will look as follows:

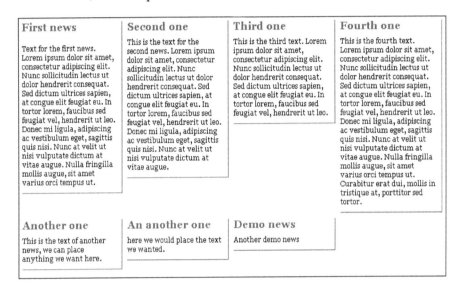

Each one of the columns has a different height, but don't worry, we are going to solve this with a bit of help from jQuery.

Equal size columns with jQuery

Having equal size columns will make our design look much better, and it's not going to be so hard. First of all, we are going to download one plugin that's going to help us with our task. Just visit this page:

`http://www.cssnewbie.com/equalheights-jquery-plugin/.`

Download the `jquery.equalheights.js` file and place it in `components/com_tinynews/js/`. In order to include it, we are going to again edit the `default.php` file to add the necessary `addScript` method:

```
...
$css = JURI::base().'components/com_tinynews/css/frontend_style.css';
$document->addStyleSheet( $css );

$js = JURI::base().'components/com_tinynews/js/
  jquery.equalheights.js';
$document->addScript($js);
```

After doing so, we need to call the plugin method; we will do that after the previous code:

```
$js = "

  jQuery(document).ready(function($){
    $('.news_box').equalHeights();
  });
";

$document->addScriptDeclaration($js);
```

The `addScriptDeclaration` method will help us add our code to the header of our site and will be executed on document ready. If we now try to reload our site, we will see that, thanks to the plugin, our columns will have exactly the same height. Want to take a look? Check the next screenshot:

First news	Second one	Third one	Fourth one
Text for the first news. Lorem ipsum dolor sit amet, consectetur adipiscing elit. Nunc sollicitudin lectus ut dolor hendrerit consequat. Sed dictum ultrices sapien, at congue elit feugiat eu. In tortor lorem, faucibus sed feugiat vel, hendrerit ut leo. Donec mi ligula, adipiscing ac vestibulum eget, sagittis quis nisi. Nunc at velit ut nisi vulputate dictum at vitae augue. Nulla fringilla mollis augue, sit amet varius orci tempus ut. Curabitur erat dui, mollis in tristique at, porttitor sed tortor.	This is the text for the second news. Lorem ipsum dolor sit amet, consectetur adipiscing elit. Nunc sollicitudin lectus ut dolor hendrerit consequat. Sed dictum ultrices sapien, at congue elit feugiat eu. In tortor lorem, faucibus sed feugiat vel, hendrerit ut leo. Donec mi ligula, adipiscing ac vestibulum eget, sagittis quis nisi. Nunc at velit ut nisi vulputate dictum at vitae augue.	This is the third text. Lorem ipsum dolor sit amet, consectetur adipiscing elit. Nunc sollicitudin lectus ut dolor hendrerit consequat. Sed dictum ultrices sapien, at congue elit feugiat eu. In tortor lorem, faucibus sed feugiat vel, hendrerit ut leo.	This is the fourth text. Lorem ipsum dolor sit amet, consectetur adipiscing elit. Nunc sollicitudin lectus ut dolor hendrerit consequat. Sed dictum ultrices sapien, at congue elit feugiat eu. In tortor lorem, faucibus sed feugiat vel, hendrerit ut leo. Donec mi ligula, adipiscing ac vestibulum eget, sagittis quis nisi. Nunc at velit ut nisi vulputate dictum at vitae augue. Nulla fringilla mollis augue, sit amet varius orci tempus ut. Curabitur erat dui, mollis in tristique at, porttitor sed tortor.

Why don't you try it on your own site? As you have seen, it's quite easy to accomplish. Also, don't forget to check the plugin's author website (http://www.cssnewbie.com/equalheights-jquery-plugin/) as there are some other interesting options that you can use:

As always, you can find these two files in the equal_heights folder of the code bundle for Chapter 9. Take a look at the folder in order to see the necessary changes. Of course, you will need to download the plugin.

Paginating our contents

Now that we have our columns with equal heights, what can we do to enhance our component? Well, as the section title itself is quite self-explanatory, I think the surprise effect has been lost.

But don't worry, to compensate, we will see a very interesting plugin; just keep reading. This time we are going to use the Quick Paginate plugin. As always, you can find it by searching on the http://jquery.com/ page or by browsing to this link:

http://plugins.jquery.com/project/quick_paginate.

After downloading the plugin, we need to place it in our js folder, components/com_tinynews/js/jquery.quickpaginate.js. Soon we will be seeing how versatile this plugin is. But first, we need to include it in our components/com_tinynews/views/tinynews/tmpl/default.php file. To do this, we will add the following code:

```
$js = JURI::base().'components/com_tinynews/js/
   jquery.quickpaginate.js';
$document->addScript($js);
```

And now it's time to change the code that we use for our addScriptDeclaration method. In our first example, we are going to make the call for quickpaginate in its default way:

```
jQuery(document).ready(function($){
  $('.news_box').equalHeights();
  $('#news_container div').quickpaginate({ perpage: 4,
     showcounter: true, pager : $('#news_container_page') });
});
";
$document->addScriptDeclaration($js);
```

We will take a look at the options in the call. But first, we will finish the example so that later, when we have a working copy, we can make changes and see the results.

Our next necessary step is going to be to create a container for our `news_box` DIVs and another one for the pagination elements. Take a look at the following code:

```
<div id="news_container">
  <?php
  foreach($this->news as $new){
  ?>
    <div class="news_box">
      <h1><?php echo $new->title; ?></h1>
      <p><?php echo $new->text; ?></p>
    </div>
  <?php
  }
  ?>
</div>

<div id="news_container_page"> </div>
```

As you can see from the previous code, we have created a `news_container` DIV that will contain all the other DIVs created in the `foreach` loop. And at the end, we have `news_container_page` that will contain the paginator elements.

Some styles are also needed and we need to add them to our `frontend_style.css` file. In fact, we are only going to add the following style:

```
#news_container_page{
    float: none;
    clear: both;
    text-align: center;
}
```

If the `jquery.quickpaginate.js` plugin is not working, we will need to make one small change to it. Open the `jquery.quickpaginate.js` file and look for the following line:

```
var pagerNav = $('<a class="'+settings.prev+'" href="#">&laquo;
Prev</a><a class="'+settings.next+'" href="#">Next &raquo;</a>');
```

Change it to:

```
var pagerNav = jQuery('<a class="'+settings.prev+'" href="#">&laquo;
Prev</a><a class="'+settings.next+'" href="#">Next &raquo;</a>');
```

Remember that we are using the SC jQuery Joomla! plugin so that our library doesn't conflict with any other library, such as MooTools. Because of that, the $ is not directly available, and so we have to use jQuery instead.

With all these elements in place, we can take a look at our site. The next screenshot shows us the output:

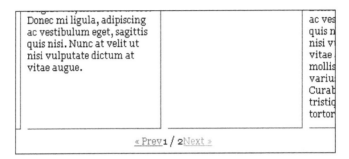

Good, we are now able to go from one page to another in just one click. Nice, isn't it?

 As in the previous topics, you can find the changes we have made in the code bundle in a folder called paginate.

And before continuing, let's take a look at the options of our call (discussed previously):

```
$('#news_container div').quickpaginate({ perpage: 4,
    showcounter: true, pager : $('#news_container_page') });
```

The options are as follows:

- perpage — defines the number of elements we want to have in each page
- showcounter — is a very useful option that not only shows the number of pages, but also the page that we are on
- pager — defines where pagination elements can be placed

However, we can also change the classes for styling the elements. Take a look at the following plugin page to see the options:

http://projects.allmarkedup.com/jquery_quick_paginate/.

Going back to the admin zone

Now, back in the admin zone we can add some interesting features to make the component admin zone easier to use.

Adding tips and instructions to fill our form using JavaScript

Adding tips and instructions may not seem so important in our component, as we only have two fields: one for the title and the other for the text. But in many forms out there, some help may be very useful while filling the form.

We are going to add some notes inside these two fields for users to see what they must write. Usually, we will do that more or less as follows:

```
<input class="text_area" type="text" name="title" id="title"
value="Sample text here" size="40"/>
```

However, we would face some problems if we were to use this approach. For example, if users write something and then delete it, the note won't appear again. This is something that isn't so important, but wouldn't it be better if the note would appear again if there is no text present in the input? Sure, and that's what we are going to do.

We can find some information regarding when to use the plugin at the following link:

```
http://manuelboy.de/projekte/jquery-formtips/
```

After downloading the plugin, we are going to place the `jquery.formtips.1.2.js` file in `administrator/components/com_tinynews/js/`, and then we are ready to go. Open the `administrator/components/com_tinynews/views/addnews/tmpl/form.php` file, and enter the following code:

```
$document->addScript($js);

$js = JURI::base().'components/com_tinynews/js/jquery.
formtips.1.2.js';
$document->addScript($js);
```

This is the same code that we always use. However, we now need to make some changes to the form's input elements so that the plugin works correctly. For example, this is our first input field:

```
<input class="text_area" type="text" name="title" id="title"
  value="<?php echo $this->news->title;?>" size="40"/>
```

The plugin needs to have a `title` element, which will contain the text that will be placed inside. For example:

```
<input class="text_area" type="text" name="title" id="title"
   value="<?php echo $this->news->title;?>" size="40"
   title="Write your title here"/>
```

We are going to do the same with our `textarea` element, as follows:

```
<textarea class="text_area" type="text" name="text" id="text"
   cols="40" rows="5" title="Write the news' text here">
   <?php echo $this->news->text;?></textarea>
```

Now we are going to make the plugin's function call, as follows:

```
jQuery(document).ready(function($){

   $('textarea').simpleautogrow();

      $('input,textarea').formtips({
            tippedClass: 'note'
         });

});
```

The only parameter we need to pass to the `formtips` function is the class the tips are going to use so that we can style them. We are going to use a class called `note`, which will look like this:

```
.note{
   color: #9A0000;
}
```

We will place this class in our `administrator/components/com_tinynews/css/styles.css` file. However, we also need to call this file in our `administrator/components/com_tinynews/views/addnews/tmpl/form.php` file:

```
$css = JURI::base().'components/com_tinynews/css/styles.css';
$document->addStyleSheet( $css );
?>
<?php defined('_JEXEC') or die('Restricted access'); ?>
```

Want to see the result? Take a look at the following screenshot:

Of course, when we try to write inside these fields the text will disappear, and when we leave the field, if we haven't written anything, our note will be placed again.

> When the form is sent, if the plugin finds that the value of the fields is equal to the notes that we have placed, it will remove these values. So, when the values reach the server, these will be empty. This way, we will know whether the user has written anything or has left the inputs empty.

You can check the changes required in the `form_notes` folder of the code bundle.

Uploading images

Wouldn't it be great to have images along our news? Surely an image would help make our component even more interesting. In this section, we are going to accomplish just that by enhancing our component to upload images.

Our first stop is going to be the `form.php` file, which we can find in `administrator/components/com_tinynews/views/addnews/tmpl/`. We need to introduce some changes to this file.

The first and foremost change is to add `enctype="multipart/form-data"` to our form declaration so that we can upload files. Without this, no upload will take place. We just need to add the following code:

```
<form action="index.php" method="post" name="adminForm"
    id="adminForm" enctype="multipart/form-data">
```

But we will also need to add an input for the file:

```
<tr>
    <td width="100" align="right" class="key">
        <label for="title">
            Image:
```

```
                        </label>
                    </td>
                    <td>
                        <input class="text_area" type="file" name="image"
                            id="file"/>
                    </td>
                </tr>
            </table>
```

Anyway, as we are changing our form, we are also going to add a caption for this image, just like this:

```
        <tr>
            <td width="100" align="right" class="key">
                <label for="title">
                    Image caption:
                </label>
            </td>
            <td>
                <input class="text_area" type="text" name="caption"
                    id="caption" value="<?php echo $this->news->caption;?>"
                    size="40" title="Write your image caption here"/>
            </td>
        </tr>
```

But if we want to save these new fields, we need to change our database table to reflect the changes. We will execute a query as follows:

```
ALTER TABLE `jos_tinynews` ADD `image` VARCHAR ( 255 ) NOT NULL ,
ADD `caption` VARCHAR ( 255 ) NOT NULL ;
```

Changing the table will let us save the fields in the database, but if you remember, we also have a table file in `administrator/components/com_tinynews/tables/addnews.php`:

```
var $id = null;
var $title = null;
var $text = null;
var $image = null;
var $caption = null;
```

The code that is highlighted represents the new fields added to our table file. With these changes, we are almost done now. However, before continuing, we are going to create a new folder where we will put the images.

This folder will be placed in `administrator/components/com_tinynews` and will be called `images`. Also, make sure to give enough permissions to the folder. 777 should work for the example, though in a real-world production environment 644 would be enough.

Our last step is to modify our model file in `administrator/components/com_tinynews/models/addnews.php`. Here we will work with the `savedata` method:

```
function savedata(){
        $row =& $this->getTable('addnews');

        if(!empty($_FILES["image"]["tmp_name"])){
          move_uploaded_file($_FILES["image"]["tmp_name"],
          $_SERVER["DOCUMENT_ROOT"].DS."administrator"
          .DS."components".DS."com_tinynews"
          .DS."images".DS.$_FILES["image"]["name"]);
        }

        $data = array();
        $data['id'] = JRequest::getVar( 'id', 'null' );
        $data['title'] = JRequest::getVar( 'title', 'null' );
        $data['text'] = JRequest::getVar( 'text', 'null' );
        $data['image'] = (!empty($_FILES["image"]["tmp_name"])  ?
        $_FILES["image"]["name"] : "");
        $data['caption'] = JRequest::getVar( 'caption', 'null' );

        if (!$row->bind( $data )) {
            $this->setError($this->_db->getErrorMsg());
            return false;
        }
}
```

Many changes have been made here. First we check if a file has been correctly uploaded:

```
if(!empty($_FILES["image"]["tmp_name"])){
```

If we have a file, we move it to our `images` folder. Note that we have used the DS constant for the separator, instead of just using / or \, which may give problems depending on the system we are working on.

Also, note something interesting. Before we had the following line:

```
if (!$row->bind( JRequest::get( 'post' ) )) {
```

And now, we have something quite different, as shown next:

```
$data = array();
$data['id'] = JRequest::getVar( 'id', 'null' );
$data['title'] = JRequest::getVar( 'title', 'null' );
$data['text'] = JRequest::getVar( 'text', 'null' );
$data['image'] = (!empty($_FILES["image"]["tmp_name"])   ?
                   $_FILES["image"]["name"] : "");
$data['caption'] = JRequest::getVar( 'caption', 'null' );

if (!$row->bind( $data )) {
```

Instead of getting the `post` array directly, we are creating our very own array. This way we can modify the value of the `image` variable, otherwise this value would be empty.

Note that many things could be improved here, but for now we will continue, just to concentrate on the jQuery part of things.

 But before we continue, why don't you take a look at the code bundle. All the changes we have made are in the `upload_images` folder.

Now that we can upload images, it would be great to show them in the frontend. The next section will be just about that.

Showing our images in the frontend

Of course, having our images uploaded is just the first step, now we need to show these images, but this is not going to be that hard. Open the `components/com_tinynews/views/tinynews/tmpl/default.php` file, and add the following code:

```
<div class="news_box">

  <?php
    if(!empty($new->image)){

  ?>
      <img src="<?php JURI::base(); ?>administrator/components/
      com_tinynews/images/<?php echo $new->image; ?>"
      alt="<?php echo $new->caption; ?>" width="165px"/>
       <p><?php echo $new->caption; ?></p>
```

```php
<?php
  }
?>


<h1><?php echo $new->title; ?></h1>
```

First, if we have some data in the image field, we prepare the `img` tag. Note that after the `JURI::base();` method we have added `administrator`, but when we were working in the admin part, this wasn't needed. The `JURI::base();` method will distinguish where we are.

At this point, with the images included, our site will look better. The next screenshot is only a demo:

An interesting way to show the caption

In this section, we will make our captions interesting. At present, they are placed in a very basic way. And, of course, we are here to make things a lot more interesting as possible.

For this we will need to make some changes to our code and of course add some jQuery. The result is going to be similar to the effect we can find at the following link:

```
http://buildinternet.com/2009/03/sliding-boxes-and-captions-with-
jquery/.
```

We will start working right away. We are going to the HTML first, as we should have the required file, `default.php`, already opened. If not, you can find it in `components/com_tinynews/views/tinynews/tmpl/default.php`:

```php
...
<?php
  if(!empty($new->image)){
?>

    <div class="news_image">
      <img src="<?php JURI::base(); ?>administrator/components/
        com_tinynews/images/<?php echo $new->image; ?>"
       alt="<?php echo $new->caption; ?>" width="165"/>
      <div class="caption">
        <p><?php echo $new->caption; ?></p>
      </div>
    </div>

<?php
  }
?>
...
```

The code is mostly the same, but we have added two DIVs: one that will contain the image and the caption and the other only for the caption. We will put these two DIVs to good use very soon.

The addition of these two DIVs will make it necessary for another change. We need to change the following code:

```
$('#news_container div').quickpaginate({ perpage: 4, showcounter:
true, pager : $('#news_container_page') });
```

The new code should be as follows:

```
$('#news_container div.news_box').quickpaginate({ perpage: 4,
showcounter: true, pager : $('#news_container_page') });
```

Previously, we didn't need to distinguish between DIVs for our pagination. Now, as we have created some more DIVs, we need to distinguish between them.

Having created the DIVs, we need to add the style, and we will do that in the `components/com_tinynews/css/frontend_style.css` file:

```css
.news_image{
  width: 165px;
  height: 76px;
  margin-bottom: 5px;
```

```
    background-color:#9A0000;
    color: #ffffff;
    overflow: hidden;
    position: relative;
}

.news_image img{
    position: absolute;
    top: 0;
    left: 0;
    border: 0;
}

.caption{
    padding: 10px;
}
```

We can see some basic styles here, the first being the container with the size of the image we want to put in it, the next being the image, and the last a padding for the caption container.

With these styles added, we have enough CSS styles for now. Go back to the `components/com_tinynews/views/tinynews/tmpl/default.php` file. We will add the following code:

```
...
$('.news_box').equalHeights();
$('#news_container div.news_box').quickpaginate({ perpage: 4,
    showcounter: true, pager : $('#news_container_page') });

$('.news_image').hover(function(){
    $('img', this).stop().animate({top:'76px'},{duration:160});
}, function() {
    $('img', this).stop().animate({top:'0px'},{duration:160});
});
```

I've highlighted the new code and the rest of the code is only for reference. This little piece of code will make things move. As you can see we are targeting every `.news_image` element. We have added the `hover` function to each element, and inside it we have two other functions.

The first one will be called when the mouse pointer enters the element and the other when the mouse pointer moves out of it. These two functions are very similar, and they make use of the `animate` function. Let's take a look at the first function:

```
$('img', this).stop().animate({top:'76px'},{duration:160});
```

Here we target the `img` element inside the `.news_image` DIV. However, it is important to note the `this` element because if we target the current element without the `this`, all elements will be target.

Then we use `stop` to make sure that no other animations are being done at the moment. Next, we use the `animate` function to move the image to the top.

This code is fun to try, and this time it would be great if you could give it a go. Meanwhile, the following screenshot shows the result:

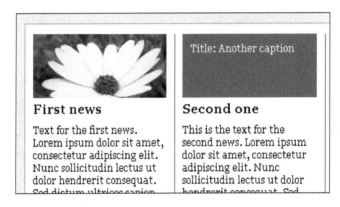

The first image looks exactly as before, but to the right, you can see another image. However, with the mouse pointer hovering over it, the effect looks much better when seeing it in a browser.

If you want to give it a try quickly, you can find the modified files inside the `image_hover` folder in the code bundle.

Adding a fresh full image pop-up script

If you remember, when we inserted the image we didn't limit its size. However, on the frontend, we are forcing the image to be smaller. Wouldn't it be great if our users can see the full-sized image? Sure it would be, and that's what we are going to do.

In the earlier chapters, we have used some image pop-up plugins. But the one we are going to use now is quite different. I'm sure you are going to like it a lot, as it will add a touch of freshness to our site.

Good, first take a look at the plugin site:

`http://herr-schuessler.de/blog/jquery-popeye-1-0-released/`.

However, you can also find the plugin on the jQuery site by searching for popeye, or by using the following link if you prefer:

`http://plugins.jquery.com/project/popeye.`

First, download the plugin. Inside the packed file, we can find a folder called `lib`. We will take the `jquery.popeye-1.0.js` file from this folder, and copy it into our own `components/com_tinynews/js` folder.

> Note that there's also a minified version. We can use this one instead, as in a production site it would be better. For development, I usually prefer not to use minified ones, just in case I would like to take a look at the plugin code.

When we have the plugin in place, we can continue with the preparative. What we will need more of are some CSS files. There are some demo files in the `css` folder of the packed file we have downloaded.

In fact, there are two CSS files:

- `jquery.popeye.css` — are the basic styles needed for the plugin to work
- `jquery.popeye.style.css` — are sample styles to determine the plugin's look and feel

As we also need to use these two files, we are going to put them in our own CSS folder, that is, `components/com_tinynews/css`.

The plugin also makes use of some images, and we need to provide them too. They are placed in the `gfx` folder. We are going to copy the entire folder into our component folder, that is, `components/com_tinynews/gfx`.

Now we can start working on the code. This time we are going to create a detail screen for our news. Therefore, we will see a page with all the news, and then a "read more" link for the fully detailed news, where we will use this new plugin.

We will edit the `components/com_tinynews/views/tinynews/tmpl/default.php` file:

```
<h1><?php echo $new->title; ?></h1>
<p><?php echo substr($new->text,0,256); ?></p>
<p><a href="<?php JURI::base() ?>
    index.php?option=com_tinynews&task=detail&id=<?php echo
    $new->id; ?>">Read more</a></p>
```

We will use the `substr` method to limit the amount of text we want to show so that we have something new to show in the detailed view. Then we create a "read more" link, passing a task called `detail` and the ID of the element.

Next, changes are needed in the `components/com_tinynews/tinynews.php` file. We will change the following line:

```
$controller->execute($task = null);
```

The changed code will be as follows:

```
$controller->execute( JRequest::getVar( 'task', 'null' ) );

$controller->redirect();
```

As earlier, our component did not need to retrieve a task; we always defined it to null. However, now it's really necessary to catch the variable.

Now that we have prepared the `tinynews.php` file, it can retrieve the task. We need to create the task in our controller. Open the `components/com_tinynews/controller.php` file because we are going to add a new, detailed method there, as follows:

```php
function detail(){
    JRequest::setVar( 'view', 'detailed' );
    JRequest::setVar( 'layout', 'default'  );

   parent::display();
}
```

Here we define the view we want to use, `detailed`, and the layout for that view, `default`. And, as we have defined a view and a template, we need to create these two files. Let's first create the view file, `view.html.php`, in `components/com_tinynews/views/detailed/`, as follows:

```php
<?php
defined( '_JEXEC' ) or die( 'Restricted access' );

jimport( 'joomla.application.component.view');

class TinynewsViewDetailed extends JView{

    function display(){

        $model =& $this->getModel();
```

```
                $news = $model->getnews();
                $this->assignRef('news', $news);
                parent::display();
        }
    }
```

There is nothing especially new here; we define the class and the default display method, and then get an instance to the model, as we need to retrieve some data from the database.

We are going to do just that with the getnews method, and then we will assign the retrieved data to the news variable.

As I mentioned before, we were going to create the view and the template. The view is just done, but before going to the template we are going to prepare the model with the necessary getnews method.

Create the detailed.php file in components/com_tinynews/models. Remember that, by default, the view loads the model called by the same name. The model content is as follows:

```php
<?php

defined( '_JEXEC' ) or die( 'Restricted access' );

jimport( 'joomla.application.component.model' );

class TinynewsModelDetailed extends JModel{

    function getnews(){

      $id = JRequest::getVar( 'id', 'null' );

        $query = ' SELECT * FROM #__tinynews WHERE id = '.$id;
        $this->_db->setQuery( $query );
        $data = $this->_db->loadObject();

        if (!$data) {
            $data = new stdClass();
            $data->id = 0;
            $data->title = null;
            $data->text = null;
            $data->image = null;
```

```
            $data->caption = null;
        }
        return $data;
    }
}
```

Here we define the `getnews` method, and inside this method we get the `id` variable we defined previously in our link, to know which record to retrieve. We execute the proper query and return the necessary values.

These values, thanks to our view, will be available in our template file, `components/com_tinynews/views/detailed/tmpl/default.php`, which is the next file to be created, as follows:

```php
<?php

defined('_JEXEC') or die('Restricted access');

$document =& JFactory::getDocument();

$css = JURI::base().'components/com_tinynews/css/frontend_style.css';
$document->addStyleSheet( $css );
$css = JURI::base().'components/com_tinynews/css/jquery.popeye.css';
$document->addStyleSheet( $css );
$css = JURI::base().'components/com_tinynews/css/
   jquery.popeye.style.css';
$document->addStyleSheet( $css );
```

In this first part, we load the necessary CSS files: our very own `frontend_style.css` and the two necessary for the plugin—`jquery.popeye.css` and `jquery.popeye.style.css`. After this goes the JavaScript, as follows:

```javascript
$js = JURI::base().'components/com_tinynews/js/jquery.popeye-1.0.js';
$document->addScript($js);

$js = "
  jQuery(document).ready(function($){
    $('#popeye1').popeye();
  });
";
$document->addScriptDeclaration($js);

?>
```

Here we load the plugin, and then we make a call to the plugin function:

```
$('#popeye1').popeye();
```

Having this in place, we can start placing some HTML, but first we get the variable prepared in the view, as follows:

```
<div id="news_container">

  <?php
    $news = $this->news;
  ?>
```

We create a `$news` variable, which will help us when using the variable. For example, when showing the title:

```
<h1><?php echo $news->title; ?></h1>
<p>
```

Now, create the HTML necessary for the plugin, as follows:

```
          <?php
            if(!empty($news->image)){
          ?>
          <div style="clear:both;">
              <div id="popeye1">
                  <ul>
                      <li><a href="<?php JURI::base(); ?>administrator/
                          components/com_tinynews/images/
                          <?php echo $news->image; ?>"><img src="<?php
                          JURI::base(); ?>administrator/components/
                          com_tinynews/images/<?php echo $news->image; ?>"
                          alt="<?php echo $news->caption; ?>"
                          width="200"/></a>
                      </li>
                  </ul>
              </div>
          </div>
          <?php
            }
          ?>
```

As we did previously, we check if the image exits. Next we place the necessary HTML, especially the `popeye1` DIV we were referencing previously, in our JavaScript code. Inside it, we have an unordered list with a list of elements.

Although in our example we only have one image, the plugin supports having more, which we can place by creating more `li` elements.

Inside each `li` element we have a link with an `href` pointing to the full-size image, and inside the `href`, a thumbnail to be used for clicking.

The final elements will be the text of the news and a return link, as follows:

```
<?php echo nl2br($news->text); ?>
<br/><br/>
</p>


<p><a href="<?php JURI::base() ?>index.php?option=com_tinynews">
    Back to all the news</a></p>
</div>
```

And the file is done. I will put some images so that we can see the result of all this work. The result is seen in the following screenshot:

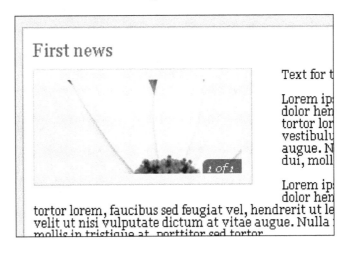

This is the default look and feel of our image. It is placed within the text with an indication of the number of images available.

Now we will see a screenshot representing what happens when we place the mouse pointer over the image:

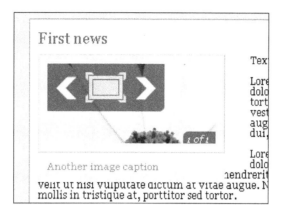

Here we can see the caption for the image, the buttons that let us see the next or previous image in case there were more images, and the expand image button. If we click on the expand image button, we will see something similar to the following screenshot:

The full-sized image is placed just over the text. Nice, isn't it? Clicking on the image again will make it small. Of course, all of this is accomplished with a nice growing effect.

All the code we have been working on, except for the plugin, which you must download, can be found in the code bundle, inside the popeye folder. Take a look at it and give the plugin a try.

The plugin has many other options and possibilities. Take a look at these at the following link:

`http://herr-schuessler.de/blog/jquery-popeye-1-0-released/`.

If you have trouble with the popeye script interfering with the main menu, for example, if the popeye image appears on top of the drop-down submenus, you can solve it by modifying the CSS of the menu. It can be found in the template's `jj15/css/menu.css` file. Modify the following code:

```
.menu{
  margin-top: -3px;
  margin-left: -15px;
}
```

The modified code is as follows:

```
.menu{
  margin-top: -3px;
  margin-left: -15px;
  z-index: 9999;
  position: absolute;
}
```

But do this modification only if the popeye script interferes with the menu, as otherwise it's not necessary.

Adding a WYSIWYG editor to our component backend

At the moment, in our component's backend, when adding or editing a new element, we have a simple textarea to do it. We enhanced this textarea to grow, as needed, when text was entered in it. But, what if we want to do something more with it, such as adding images, links, bold text, and so on?

For this we could use a WYSIWYG editor. **WYSIWYG** stands for **What You See Is What You Get**, and if you have been using Joomla!, you surely will have seen one.

We can add a jQuery editor plugin, much in the same way that we added the textarea autogrow script. However, this is quite easy, and I think it would be more interesting to see how to use Joomla!'s editor.

First, open the `administrator/components/com_tinynews/views/addnews/tmpl/form.php` file. In this file, we will remove the simpleautogrow plugin because it won't work together with the WYSIWYG editor. Remove the next piece of code, except for the highlighted line, which is still needed:

```
$js = JURI::base().'components/com_tinynews/js/
    jquery.simpleautogrow.js';
$document =& JFactory::getDocument();
$document->addScript($js);
```

Also, remove the following line:

```
$('textarea').simpleautogrow();
```

Now search for the following code:

```
<textarea class="text_area" type="text" name="text" id="text"
cols="40" rows="5" title="Write the news' text here"><?php echo
$this->news->text;?></textarea>
```

This was the code we used to create our textarea. We will change it as follows:

```
<?php
 $editor =& JFactory::getEditor();echo $editor->display('text',
        $this->news->text, '550', '400', '60', '20');
?>
```

This will generate an editor just like the one you can see in the following screenshot:

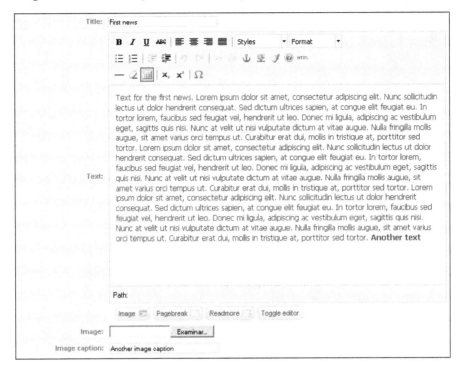

Let's take a look into the parameters we used to create it:

```
echo $editor->display(the element name as in any other input,
                the value, width, height, columns, rows);
```

Now, if we try to write text and save it, we will see that it works, and our text is saved just as when we worked with a textarea. However, if we add some HTML code, like some bold text for example, the HTML won't be saved. That's a security measure. All HTML is removed before our text is inserted in the database.

But we want our HTML to be saved. So open the `administrator/components/com_tinynews/models/addnews.php` file and search for this line:

```
$data['text'] = JRequest::getVar( 'text', 'null' );
```

Change it as follows:

```
$data['text'] = JRequest::getVar( 'text', 'null', 'post', 'string',
                JREQUEST_ALLOWRAW );
```

The post and string parameters are not the important parts here, though they are useful to tell us that we are receiving the value from the POST array, and that we expect a string value.

The last parameter, JREQUEST_ALLOWRAW, will be the most important one, as it will tell Joomla! to not remove the HTML. The exact value of the variable will be put into the database, text, and HTML.

And we are done! With this we have a complete WYSIWYG editor available in our component.

 You can find the modifications we made in the code bundle in the wysiwyg folder.

Summary

We have reached the final point of the chapter; hope you had a good time reading it. We have seen quite a lot of things in it. However, the most important fact is that we can take a plain component and enhance it by using jQuery plugins to achieve a very interesting result.

Some of the plugins we have used, such as the textarea autogrow, form tips, and the equal size columns, are not visually impressive, but help us make our site more usable and appealing to the users.

Others, such as pagination plugin, are very important these days, as they greatly enhance the usability of our component. Lastly, we have used an image plugin; these are visually appealing, and so our component looks really good.

Of course, the component can be further enhanced. However, maybe the things we have seen in the chapter have given you some ideas. Just take the component code and try to modify it and add your favourite plugins to it.

10
Problems and Usability

"Errors are inherent to development, so we must be prepared."

In this last chapter, I've something interesting in mind. We are going to see how to prepare our code for problems such as not having JavaScript enabled, and take a look at how we can we make our code work with MooTools. We will also take a quick look at how to use Firebug in a particular scenario. We can summarize the topics in this chapter into the following points:

- What happens if JavaScript is disabled?
- Using Firebug to help us in our development
- Possible problems and solutions with jQuery
- Optimizing CSS and JavaScript

I think all these topics are very interesting, and as a final chapter, I want all of us to have a great time while working on the final aspects of our site.

What happens if JavaScript is disabled?

This is something we should always take care of, as most of our visitors may have JavaScript disabled in their browsers. Throughout this book we haven't had enough time to take a look at it. So I hope that in this example we can take a look at the main aspects of this problem.

For this example, we are going to use a new little module called `mod_tinyphotos`. You can find the `mod_tinyphotos.tar.gz` file in the code bundle of Chapter 10 and at this point it's more or less in the middle of its development. It will be perfect for us then because we can practice with it. But first we need to install it, and as always, we can do that in our administrator screen from **Extensions | Install/Uninstall**.

Once we have our module installed, we can see it as a module called **Tiny Photos**, with all of our other modules in **Extensions | Module Manager**, as shown in the following screenshot:

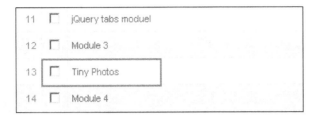

Of course, we need to enable the Tiny Photos module and place it in the module position we want. For this example, **module_3** of our template is the position used. Once the module is enabled, it will appear on our page, using the photos introduced in our tinynews component. It will look like the following screenshot:

Of course, much work needs to be done for this module to be finished, but it will serve us as a starting point. As we can see these are the images of our news. I have put one image in each bit of news, so we have all the necessary images.

We need something more—a jQuery plugin. This time we are going to use a plugin called jCarousel from Jan Sorgalla, which can be found at:

http://sorgalla.com/projects/jcarousel/.

This plugin is going to help us create a nice carousel effect from our images. So let's download it and see how we can, in a very basic way, make it work.

Once the plugin is downloaded, we need to move some files into our module installation. The first file we are going to need is jquery.jcarousel.pack.js, which we will place in modules/mod_tinyphotos/js. Of course, we need to include it in our modules/mod_tinyphotos/mod_tinyphotos.php file, as shown in the following piece of code:

```
JHTML::stylesheet('styles.css','modules/mod_tinyphotos/css/');

$document =& JFactory::getDocument();
$document->addScript(JURI::root(true).'modules'.DS.'mod_tinyphotos'
        .DS.'js'.DS.'jquery.jcarousel.pack.js');
```

We will also need to add some CSS files. First among them is the `jquery.jcarousel.css` file that we will place in the `modules/mod_tinyphotos/css` folder. But we will also need to include it in our `mod_tinyphotos.php` file, just as we did before. Take a look at the code required; it is as follows:

```
JHTML::stylesheet('jquery.jcarousel.css','modules/
                  mod_tinyphotos/css/');
```

This file has the basic necessary styles for the plugin to work, but we also need one skin CSS file and its folder. The skin will include some images and other elements to make the carousel look better. We are going to use the default one, so copy the `tango` folder in `modules/mod_tinyphotos/css`, and then include the CSS file of the skin in the `mod_tinyphotos.php` file:

```
JHTML::stylesheet('skin.css','modules/mod_tinyphotos/css/tango/');
```

Now we only need to invoke the plugin function. We will do that at the end of the `modules/mod_tinyphotos/tmpl/default_tmpl.php` file:

```
...
   </ul>

</div>

<script type="text/javascript">

  jQuery(document).ready(function() {
      jQuery('#carousel').jcarousel();
  });

</script>
```

This will result in our module looking just as shown in the following screenshot:

We still need to do some modifications, mostly style modifications, which we will be including in the `modules/mod_tinyphotos/css/styles.css` file as follows:

```css
.jcarousel-skin-tango .jcarousel-container {
    -moz-border-radius: 0;
    background: transparent;
    border: 0;
}

.jcarousel-skin-tango .jcarousel-container-horizontal {
    width: 835px;
    padding: 10px 40px;
}

.jcarousel-skin-tango .jcarousel-clip-horizontal {
    width:   835px;
    height: 70px;
}

.jcarousel-skin-tango .jcarousel-item {
    width: 150px;
    height: 70px;
}

.jcarousel-skin-tango .jcarousel-next-horizontal, .jcarousel-skin-tango .jcarousel-prev-horizontal {
    top: 32px;
}
```

Remember that for these modifications to work, we need to load our CSS file after the plugin's CSS file. This way our styles will prevail and modify the styles found in the plugin's own CSS file. You can see how this is done in the following code:

```
JHTML::stylesheet('jquery.jcarousel.css','modules/mod_
tinyphotos/css/');

JHTML::stylesheet('skin.css','modules/mod_tinyphotos/
css/tango/');

JHTML::stylesheet('styles.css','modules/mod_
tinyphotos/css/');
```

With our styles added, our module will look as follows:

This looks better now, and it has been quite easy to achieve, thanks to the jCarousel plugin. But how would this look without jQuery? The answer is like the next screenshot:

This is not very useful, as our visitors won't be able to see all the images. How can we improve this? Well, in fact quite easily, thanks to the noscript HTML tag. Remember our modules/mod_tinyphotos/tmpl/default_tmpl.php file? In this file, we have the following code:

```
<script type="text/javascript">

    jQuery(document).ready(function() {
        jQuery('#carousel').jcarousel();
    });

</script>
```

Just after this code we are going to place this code:

```
<noscript>
  <style>
    #tinyphotos{
      width: 892px;
      height: 90px;
      overflow: auto;
    }

    #tinyphotos ul{
      width: <?php echo (165 * $i); ?>px
    }
  </style>
</noscript>
```

The code placed inside the `noscript` tag will be executed only when JavaScript is not enabled. This code will give our `tinyphotos` DIV an overflow property, which will show a scrollbar when needed.

Next our tinyphotos `ul` element will be given a width equivalent to that of all our images. We need to calculate this width and do it before the styles declared inside the `noscript` tag we have just written. It is quite easily done in our `foreach` loop:

```php
<?php
  $i=0;
  foreach($news as $new){
  ?>

    <li><img src="<?php JURI::base(); ?>administrator/components/
      com_tinynews/images/<?php echo $new->image; ?>" alt="<?php echo
      $new->caption; ?>" height="70"/></li>

  <?php
    $i++;
  }
?>

  </ul>
```

That way we know the width necessary, so all images are correctly placed inside our `ul` element. The result, while not as nice as the JavaScript version, is much better than having nothing applied at all. Take a look at the next screenshot to see the difference:

This way, even with JavaScript disabled, our visitors are able to see our images.

In order to check a site with JavaScript disabled, you can download Web Developer, which is a Firefox add-on. This useful extension will be of great help in all your developments, so give it a try.

Remember that you can download all this code from the code bundle, except for the jQuery plugin, which you must download from its author's site:

`http://sorgalla.com/projects/jcarousel/`.

The folder for these changes can be found in the `mod_tinyphotos_changes` folder.

Another example: mod_littlecontact

`mod_littlecontact` is also quite easy to modify, so it can work with or without JavaScript enabled. For example, in our `modules/mod_littlecontact/tmpl/default_tmpl.php` file, we have the following line:

```
<input type="button" name="send" value="Send" class="sc_button"
id="send_button"/>
```

We will replace it with the following line:

```
<input type="submit" name="send" value="Send" class="sc_button"
id="send_button"/>
```

We were using `button` instead of `submit` so that submitting the form doesn't refresh the page, loading it again. We were using jQuery to send the form, but if JavaScript is not enabled, we won't be able to send the form.

Using `submit` instead will enable the form to be sent, but we still want to send it with AJAX if JavaScript is enabled. For this, we are going to modify the `modules/mod_littlecontact/js/littlecontact.js` file.

In that file, we have the following code:

```
jQuery(document).ready(function($){
    $('#send_button').click(function() {
    //First we do some validation, just to know that we have some data
```

Now, we are going to change it to the following:

```
jQuery(document).ready(function($){

    $('#send_button').click(function(e) {
        e.preventDefault();

    //First we do some validation, just to know that we have some data
```

We use the `preventDefault` method so that the submit button is prevented from working, and we can continue with our jQuery code. This way we can easily use this method to send our form using jQuery, and if JavaScript is not enabled, the form will be sent just as any other form.

Using Firebug to help us in our development

Firebug, like the Web Developer toolbar, is another very useful extension, especially when developing JavaScript. But Firebug can be used for many other things, such as exploring the HTML or CSS of our site.

Like the previous extension, we can download this Firefox extension from the Firefox add-ons site at `https://addons.mozilla.org`.

Once installed, Firebug needs to be enabled from the add-ons screen:

Once enabled, a new button will appear at the bottom right-hand side of the Firefox browser. You will notice a tiny icon that looks like the previous icon, but smaller, as follows:

Once we click on this button, a new panel will appear with some tabs that we can see in the following screenshot:

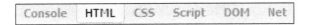

How we can use two of these tabs, **Console** and **HTML**, is something that we are just about to find out.

Using Firebug to log messages

When working with JavaScript, especially AJAX, it's quite useful to know what is happening. For example, in our `mod_littlecontact` module, we have a `click` event that is called when the button is clicked, as follows:

```
$('#send_button').click(function(e) {
```

This function in turn makes some checks and then makes the following call:

```
$.post("index.php", $("#sc_form").serialize(), show_ok());
```

This results in the `show_ok()` function being called. The problem is that when we click on the button, we have no control over which function is being executed at the time. So if something goes wrong it will be quite hard to know where the error is.

With Firebug, we have a method called `console.log`, which we can use to place some messages at some points. In our button click event, we will place something as follows:

```
$('#send_button').click(function(e) {

    console.log('The button has been clicked');
```

As you can see, we have placed the `console.log` method with one message, which informs us that the button has been clicked.

Also, in our `show_ok` function, we are going to place a similar message, like the next one:

```
function show_ok(){

    console.log('We are in the show_ok function');
```

But how do we see these messages? Well, when our page is loaded and the Firebug screen is open, you can click on the **Console** tab and will see something such as this:

We can see our messages, and this way we know our code has gone through these two functions, but we can also see the AJAX call that was made to the `index.php` file:

```
$.post("index.php", $("#sc_form").serialize(), show_ok());
```

With this small help, it's a bit easier to work with JavaScript and AJAX queries. But what about the **HTML** tab? Let's continue to take a look at that other interesting option.

Using Firebug to check HTML source code

This may seem less useful than the previous option, but soon you will see how we can use it to our own benefit.

Think about our jCarousel example; for it to work we placed the following code:

```
<div id="tinyphotos">

  <ul id="carousel" class="jcarousel-skin-tango">

<?php
  $i=0;
  foreach($news as $new){
  ?>

    <li><img src="<?php JURI::base(); ?>administrator/components/
        com_tinynews/images/<?php echo $new->image; ?>"
        alt="<?php echo $new->caption; ?>" height="70"/></li>

  <?php
    $i++;
  }
?>

  </ul>

</div>
```

Later, when our site is loaded, if we check the source code we can see the following:

```
<div id="tinyphotos">

        <ul id="carousel" class="jcarousel-skin-tango">


              <li><img src="/administrator/components/
                  com_tinynews/images/image_1.jpg"
                  alt="Another image caption" height="70"/></li>
          ...

              <li><img src="/administrator/components/
                  com_tinynews/images/image_1.jpg"
                  alt="Image with text" height="70"/></li>

        </ul>

</div>
```

However, after the jCarousel plugin is called, this code will be modified. But, if we take a look at the Firebug screen's **HTML** tab, we will see a screen where we can navigate through the code. In fact, if we start expanding the code (clicking on the plus symbols near to the code), we will find a code that looks similar to the next image:

```
<div id="tinyphotos">
    <div class=" jcarousel-skin-tango">
        <div class="jcarousel-container jcarousel-container-horizontal" style="display:
        block;">
            <div class="jcarousel-prev jcarousel-prev-horizontal jcarousel-prev-disabled
            jcarousel-prev-disabled-horizontal" style="display: block;" disabled="true">
            </div>
            <div class="jcarousel-next jcarousel-next-horizontal" style="display:
            block;" disabled="false"></div>
            <div class="jcarousel-clip jcarousel-clip-horizontal">
                <ul id="carousel" class=" jcarousel-list jcarousel-
                list-horizontal" style="width: 1280px; left: 0px;">
                    <li class="jcarousel-item jcarousel-item-horizontal jcarousel-item-1
                    jcarousel-item-1-horizontal" jcarouselindex="1">
                    <li class="jcarousel-item jcarousel-item-horizontal jcarousel-item-2
                    jcarousel-item-2-horizontal" jcarouselindex="2">
                    <li class="jcarousel-item jcarousel-item-horizontal jcarousel-item-3
                    jcarousel-item-3-horizontal" jcarouselindex="3">
                    <li class="jcarousel-item jcarousel-item-horizontal jcarousel-item-4
                    jcarousel-item-4-horizontal" jcarouselindex="4">
                    <li class="jcarousel-item jcarousel-item-horizontal jcarousel-item-5
                    jcarousel-item-5-horizontal" jcarouselindex="5">
                    <li class="jcarousel-item jcarousel-item-horizontal jcarousel-item-6
                    jcarousel-item-6-horizontal" jcarouselindex="6">
                    <li class="jcarousel-item jcarousel-item-horizontal jcarousel-item-7
                    jcarousel-item-7-horizontal" jcarouselindex="7">
                    <li class="jcarousel-item jcarousel-item-horizontal jcarousel-item-8
                    jcarousel-item-8-horizontal" jcarouselindex="8">
                </ul>
            </div>
        </div>
    </div>
</div>
```

This code is the result of our page, modified by the jCarousel plugin, with new elements and classes. It can be very useful to be able to see these modifications. But even better, if we move our mouse by the code, the elements will be highlighted, so we know in each instance which code we are looking at.

Of course, all these things are only a very little piece of what can be achieved with Firebug. If you want to learn more, you can take a look at the following link:

`http://net.tutsplus.com/tutorials/other/10-reasons-why-you-should-be-using-firebug/.`

There you will be able to see other uses of Firebug so that you can make the most of it.

Possible problems and solutions with jQuery

When working with JavaScript, we can have more problems than not having JavaScript available; for example, the called URL not being available, a timeout, or something similar.

That can be quite inconvenient for our visitors, especially if they don't know that something bad has happened. Taking our `mod_littlecontact` as an example again, this module uses the following script to make the AJAX call:

```
$.post("index.php", $("#sc_form").serialize(), show_ok());
```

Instead of writing this URL, misspell it as follows:

```
$.post("inde.php", $("#sc_form").serialize(), show_ok());
```

Well, you can give it a try, but I would like to tell you that no errors will occur. All will work as expected, except that the mail will not be sent.

This can be quite a problem when developing, as we won't really know where the error is happening. But think about our visitors; they will see the "mail sent ok" message, which is not true.

Of course, we can do something about this. For example, let's modify our `modules/mod_littlecontact/js/littlecontact.js` file just after this line of code:

```
jQuery(document).ready(function($){
```

We are going to add this little piece of JavaScript:

```
$.ajaxSetup({
  error:function(x,e){
    if(x.status==404){
      alert('URL not found.');
      }else if(e=='timeout'){
      alert('Request Time out.');
    }else {
    alert('Unknow Error.\n'+x.responseText);
    }
  }
});
```

Here we are using the `ajaxSetup` method to set default values for all AJAX calls that are going to be made—in our example, only the post one. We are defining some possible errors, and if we now try to send the form, we will see an alert as follows:

This is a good start, as now when the error happens, we see some advice. That can help us while developing, but for our visitors, it can be a bit misleading. That's because our visitors will see the error message, but in our module they will read the following:

So they will see the error alert message, but also the module saying the form has been sent okay. Anyway, I don't like alerts, as visitors may think they have done something bad. So, we are going to remove the alert and use our Firebug instead:

```
$.ajaxSetup({
  error:function(x,e){
    if(x.status==404){
      console.log('Url not found');
    }else if(e=='timeout'){
      console.log('Request timeout');
    }else {
      console.log('Unknow Error.\n'+x.responseText);
    }
  }
});
```

And the result of this code, when the form is submitted again, would be something quite similar to the next Firebug screenshot:

```
The button has been clicked
We are in the show_ok function
⊞ POST http://wayofthewebninja.com/inde.php  404 Not Found ✖  134ms
Url not found
```

Here we can see our message telling us the problem that continues to be of help for us. But what about our visitors? Let's help them. To do this we are going to modify the `ajaxSetup` method just a bit, as follows:

```
$.ajaxSetup({
  error:function(x,e){
    if(x.status==404){
      console.log('Url not found');
      show_error('There was a problem sending the form,
                  please try later.');
    }else if(e=='timeout'){
      console.log('Request timeout');
      show_error('There was a problem sending the form,
                  please try later.');
    }else {
      console.log('Unknow Error.\n'+x.responseText);
      show_error('There was a problem sending the form,
                  please try later.');
    }
  }
});
```

As we can see now, after the `console.log` call, we make a call to another function, `show_error`, which has the following code in it:

```
function show_error(message){

$("#message_sent").html("<br/><br/><br/><h1>"+message+"</h1><br/>
<br/><br/><a href='index.php' class='message_link' id='message_
back'>Back to the form</a>");

    $("#sending_message").addClass("hidden_div");
    $("#message_sent").removeClass("hidden_div");

    $("input:text").val('');
    $("textarea").val('');

}
```

This function modifies the content of the message_sent DIV, using the HTML jQuery method. So, we can show an error message to our visitors when something goes bad. They will see a message like the one in the following screenshot:

This way our visitors will know that something has gone wrong. Their form has not been sent, and they must try again, or use another way of contacting us.

Of course, there are more request states, and not just the 404. Just in case you want to take into account other possible errors, you can check them at the following URL:

http://www.w3.org/Protocols/rfc2616/rfc2616-sec10.html.

 You can find these modifications to mod_littlecontact in the code bundle for Chapter 10 in the folder called littlecontact. Give it a try!

Optimizing CSS and JavaScript

By this point in the book, our sample site will have quite a good load of JavaScript and CSS files. Each file request requires time and adds to the overall site load time. Now our site has over 20 CSS files, and more or less the same number of JavaScript files.

What can be done to reduce the number of calls? Well, as developers, we could pack our JavaScript and CSS files in as few files as possible. But as we are using lots of third-party extensions, and as it will be quite a huge task to try to pack these files, we should search for another option.

A good option will be to use a plugin like the JCH Optimize plugin, which we can find in the Joomla! Extensions Directory at the following URL:

http://extensions.joomla.org/extensions/site-management/site-performance/12088.

Once installed, this extension can be found under **Extensions | Plugin Manager**:

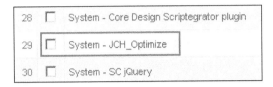

Just enable the plugin and then click on it. To edit its options, we are going to see which options are available (just the basic ones). First take a look at the next image:

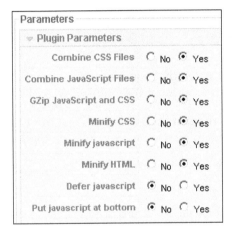

Let's talk a bit about each option.

Option	Description
Combine CSS Files	This option will merge all CSS files into just one file, so there's only one file to request.
Combine JavaScript Files	Works the same as the previous option, but for JavaScript files.
GZip JavaScript and CSS	If we have the zlib library installed in our server, our JavaScript and CSS files will be compressed so that they download faster.
Minify CSS	This will remove whitespace and comments from our CSS files. This is useful while developing, but not so useful in production.
Minify javascript	Works the same but for JavaScript files.

Option	Description
Minify HTML	Just the same as in the previous options, but for the resulting HTML code.
Defer javascript	This can be used with a bit of care, as the defer attribute indicates that our JavaScript code is not creating any elements, so it can be interpreted later. In our site, the jCarousel plugin, for example, created some HTML that would give us some problems. For our site we are not going to use this option.
Put javascript at bottom	This option places our JavaScript code at the end of the site.

Once enabled, this plugin will greatly improve the load time of our site. For example, if we take a look at the source code with the plugin disabled, we can see something like this:

```
<link rel="stylesheet" href="/modules/mod_littlecontact/css/
    styles.css" type="text/css" />
<link rel="stylesheet" href="/modules/mod_tinynews/css/
    styles.css" type="text/css" />
<link rel="stylesheet" href="/modules/mod_slider/scrollable.css"
    type="text/css" />
<link rel="stylesheet" href="/modules/mod_tinyphotos/css/
    jquery.jcarousel.css" type="text/css" />
<link rel="stylesheet" href="/modules/mod_tinyphotos/css/tango/
    skin.css" type="text/css" />
...

<script type="text/javascript" src="/plugins/system/scjquery/js/
    jquery-1.4.1.min.js"></script>
<script type="text/javascript" src="/plugins/system/scjquery/js/
    jquery.no.conflict.js"></script>
<script type="text/javascript" src="/plugins/system/scjquery/js/
    jquery-ui.min.js"></script>
<script type="text/javascript" src="/plugins/content/ppgallery/res/
    jquery.prettyPhoto.js" charset="utf-8"></script>

<script type="text/javascript" src="/modules/mod_littlecontact/js/
    littlecontact.js"></script>
. . .
```

Well I've reduced this code a lot, but, as commented on before, we have almost 40 file loads. After we enable the plugin, external file loads will reduce a lot, and if we check the source code while the plugin is enabled, we will see the following code:

```
<link rel="stylesheet" type="text/css" href="/plugins/system/JCH_
Optimize/jscss.php?f=db0e623db9e07ff434eb6e98be2f1193&amp;type=css"/>
  <script type="text/javascript" src="/plugins/system/JCH_Optimize/
jscss.php?f=a01fc003c676df3d78713c979090db9f&amp;type=js"></script>
```

These are two temporary files that will contain all the other CSS and JavaScript files, minified, and if the option is enabled, gzipped.

Of course, care must be taken when using this plugin as sometimes errors may occur. So you will need to try different options or exclude some files. Just try it! You will find it's a great tool.

Summary

Well, we have reached the end of the chapter. I hope these little tricks are of help in your development. When developing, in the measure of our possibilities we must take into account problems such as disabled JavaScript, failed AJAX calls, and many more. Firebug can be the best tool in our toolbox when talking about JavaScript development.

Though we haven't seen all the possible options in Firebug, I hope this little guide helps you a bit.

And this is the final chapter for the book, so I hope you had a great time while reading it. Packt's team and I have put in great effort while working on this book to make it of great help for you. I had a nice time writing the book, and it would be great if you would write to me with your opinion on the book, suggestions, and, of course, criticism.

Also, I would like to thank you for purchasing this book. It encourages me to put even greater efforts into my future projects.

Index

Symbols

O

onAfterDisplayContent event 52
onBeforeDisplayContent event 52
onPrepareContent event 52

P

packing 164
pagerLinks class 224
pagerLinks elements 224
Parallax effect
  adding, to template 118
  example 118
  HTML, preparing for example 119-122
  jQuery Parallax library, adding 122
Parallax plugin
  downloading 122
parameters, coda_bubble class
  BubbleImagesPath 135
  bubbletimes 135
  bubblewidths 135
  distances 135
  hidedelays 135
  leftshifts 135
  msieFix 135
  msiepop 135
parameters, Flickr Album Plugin
  album title default 60
  col count default 61
  color theme 60
  debugging comments 61
  default user 60
  enlarged size default 61
  Flickr API Key 60
  include jQuery 61
  include jQuery Flickr 61
  link text default 60
  row count default 61
  sort order default 61
  thumb border size 61
  thumb margin size 61
  thumb padding size 61
  thumb size default 60
parameters, Ninja ShadowBox
  CSS Skin 18
  enable cache 18
  fix Internet Explorer 8 18

image Map ID 18
include core JS Library 17
include JS 18
JavaScript library 17
media formats 18
Shadowbox language 18
parameters, pPGallery
  about 22
  caption 23
  fixed thumbnail spacing 22
  horizontal padding 23
  link popup text 23
  no. of thumbnails 23
  prefix text 23
  quality 23
  thumbnails only 23
  vertical padding 23
  width and height 22
parameters, SC jQuery plugin
  about 64
  Enable plugin for backend 64
  Enable plugin for frontend 64
  Enter custom code here 64
  jQuery UI theme 64
  Load jQuery UI libraries (all) 64
PixSearch Ajax Search module 47
pop-up image gallery 23
post method 155
post parameter 253
pPGallery
  downloading 21
  installing 22
  parameters 22

Q

query method 185
quote method 182

R

R3D Floater 93
ready function 155
redirect method 201
registerTask method 202
RJ_InsertCode 59
RokAjaxSearch 47

Thank you for buying
Joomla! 1.5 JavaScript jQuery

About Packt Publishing

Packt, pronounced 'packed', published its first book "*Mastering phpMyAdmin for Effective MySQL Management*" in April 2004 and subsequently continued to specialize in publishing highly focused books on specific technologies and solutions.

Our books and publications share the experiences of your fellow IT professionals in adapting and customizing today's systems, applications, and frameworks. Our solution based books give you the knowledge and power to customize the software and technologies you're using to get the job done. Packt books are more specific and less general than the IT books you have seen in the past. Our unique business model allows us to bring you more focused information, giving you more of what you need to know, and less of what you don't.

Packt is a modern, yet unique publishing company, which focuses on producing quality, cutting-edge books for communities of developers, administrators, and newbies alike. For more information, please visit our website: www.packtpub.com.

About Packt Open Source

In 2010, Packt launched two new brands, Packt Open Source and Packt Enterprise, in order to continue its focus on specialization. This book is part of the Packt Open Source brand, home to books published on software built around Open Source licences, and offering information to anybody from advanced developers to budding web designers. The Open Source brand also runs Packt's Open Source Royalty Scheme, by which Packt gives a royalty to each Open Source project about whose software a book is sold.

Writing for Packt

We welcome all inquiries from people who are interested in authoring. Book proposals should be sent to author@packtpub.com. If your book idea is still at an early stage and you would like to discuss it first before writing a formal book proposal, contact us; one of our commissioning editors will get in touch with you.

We're not just looking for published authors; if you have strong technical skills but no writing experience, our experienced editors can help you develop a writing career, or simply get some additional reward for your expertise.

Learning Joomla! 1.5 Extension Development

ISBN: 978-1-847191-30-4   Paperback: 200 pages

A practical tutorial for creating your first Joomla! 1.5 extensions with PHP

1. Program your own extensions to Joomla!

2. Create new, self-contained components with both back-end and front-end functionality

3. Create configurable site modules to show information on every page

4. Distribute your extensions to other Joomla! users

Building Websites with Joomla! 1.5

ISBN: 978-1-847195-30-2   Paperback: 384 pages

The best-selling Joomla! tutorial guide updated for the latest 1.5 release

1. Learn Joomla! 1.5 features

2. Install and customize Joomla! 1.5

3. Configure Joomla! administration

4. Create your own Joomla! templates

5. Extend Joomla! with new components, modules, and plug-ins

Please check **www.PacktPub.com** for information on our titles

Learning jQuery

ISBN: 978-1-847192-50-9   Paperback: 380 pages

Better Interaction Design and Web Development with Simple JavaScript Techniques

1. Create better, cross-platform JavaScript code

2. Learn detailed solutions to specific client-side problems

3. For web designers who want to create interactive elements for their designs

4. For developers who want to create the best user interface for their web applications.

Drupal 6 JavaScript and jQuery

ISBN: 978-1-847196-16-3   Paperback: 340 pages

Putting jQuery, AJAX, and JavaScript effects into your Drupal 6 modules and themes

1. Learn about JavaScript support in Drupal 6

2. Packed with example code ready for you to use

3. Harness the popular jQuery library to enhance your Drupal sites

4. Make the most of Drupal's built-in JavaScript libraries

Please check **www.PacktPub.com** for information on our titles